Struggling to be the Voice

Written by Nicholas Dinshaw

STRUGGLING TO BE THE VOICE

"The change was necessary not because I wanted it but because there was no growth."

© 2019 Nicholas Dinshaw. All Rights Reserved

Table of Contents

INTRODUCTION 1

CHAPTER ONE 5

The Start to Every Story 5

    FALLEN LEAVES: BEING MADE NEW 5

    THE LIGHT BEYOND THE CLOUDS 6

    ILLUSION OF LIFE 7

    ONENESS: WE ARE SPIRITS 8

    OPEN WOUNDS 9

    THE CALLING 10

    INSPIRE 11

    YOU ARE NOT YOUR EXPERIENCES 12

    HUMAN CONDITION: UNDERSTANDING STRUGGLE 14

    MIRRORING LOVE 15

    DIVINE: SOMETHING GREATER 16

    OUR SPIRITUAL JOURNEY: FAITH 17

CHAPTER TWO 19

We Are One *19*

    LABELS: FREE YOUSELF 19

    PIECES OF ME: MISSING 20

INNER VOICE..................................21
SOCIAL CONDITIONING: THE
   AUTHENTIC YOU 22
ETERNAL BEINGS............................24
UNIQUENESS...................................25
POSITIVE CHANGE SIGNIFIES GROWTH
  28
SPEAK YOUR TRUTH 29
CONFLICTED 31
REFLECTIONS.................................32
QUICK TO JUDGE..........................35
LOVE AND SUPPORT.....................36

CHAPTER THREE **39**
All That I Am *39*
I WILL NOT HURT MY ENEMY 39
PERFORMITIVITY: HANDS IN THE
   POCKET 40
PEBBLES ON THE GROUND 43
YOUR TEARS NEVER FALL......................44
RUNNING AWAY FROM FEAR................47
TRUST YOUR HEART 51
A BEACON OF LIGHT 53
WHY ARE WE HERE?.................................55

VALIDATION, AUTHENTICTY, AND KINDNESS............ 60

CHAPTER FOUR..........................63

Voiceless...............................63

HE WAS AFRAID 63
MONSTER: CONFORM PLEASE............. 65
A BROKEN HEART 66
FOLLOW YOUR HEART.......... 68
LOST ON THE NEVER ENDING BRIDGE 70
A PARTIAL RECOVERY 72
YOU ARE A BEAUTIFUL CREATION 74
FINDING OUR SENSE OF BELONGING.. 77
SURVIVOR............ 80
DO YOU SEE ME? 82
UNNOTICED 84
FAR FROM PERFECT............. 84

CHAPTER FIVE 87

Replacing the Old with the New...................87

FROM VICTIM TO SURVIVOR 87
PICKING UP THE PIECES......... 92
WRITING INSIDE YOUR HEAD............. 95
OUR STRONGEST 97
THAT DAY EVERYTHING CHANGED ... 98

TIME STANDS STILL 100
THE PATH THAT NEVER ENDS.............101
GOOD ENOUGH..102
LIMITS 104
TOXIC PEOPLE 105
WHAT IS LOVE? 108
NOBODY LOVES ME MORE THAN ME 110
INSECURITY 113

CHAPTER SIX 117
Be a Voice, Not an Echo *117*
RESTRICTIONS: IMPRISONED IN OUR MIND 117
PERFORMANCE MINDSET......................119
ELEMENTARY SCHOOL 121
SEVENTH GRADE 123
BULLIED..125
BIRTHDAY BEATS 129
SUICIDE 131
FINDING YOURSELF................................133
WHO WE ARE 135
BODY IMAGE...137
A FRESH START 138
DOCUMENTING EXPERIENCES............140

BUS FIGHTS 144
YOU NEVER BELIEVED IN ME............ 148
DEFINITIONS OF YOU 153
JEALOUSY 155
NOTICED.. 158
HEAR HIS CRY, SENSE HIS STRUGGLES 160
TELL NO ONE.. 164
CRAZY REDHEAD 166
CRA-ZZZY REDHEAD 169
CRAZY REDHEAD TO LOST 171

CHAPTER SEVEN.................................175
Wisdom in Your Words 175

RUNNING AWAY SEEMED EASIER..... 175
BROKEN FAMILIES LEAD TO BROKEN HEARTS.. 176
WISDOM FROM THE WISE.................... 179
REMEMBERING QUEENIE 183
EVERYDAY STRUGGLES 186
IT'S NEVER ENOUGH.............................. 188
DON'T TALK 191
THEY CALLED ME THE PARTY KID ... 193
TURN IT DOWN 198
YOU WILL NEVER BE ABLE TO DO IT 200

CHAPTER EIGHT 205
Whisper From Above *205*
- MAKING ME NEW 205
- CHILDREN OF THE FOREST 207
- SHINE YOUR LIGHT 209
- IT WASN'T SADNESS IT WAS ANGER .211
- THE WATER BOY 215
- REVENGE 216
- ACCEPTANCE 218
- STAND UP 222
- I HAVE TO WRITE MY TEST 224
- CHANGE ROOM 227
- THE GIRL ON THE BLEACHERS 229
- THE BOY THAT CAME TO THE STALL 233
- FRIEND OR FOE 235
- PATHS THAT CROSS 237
- *THE INFLUENCE YOU HAVE* 238

CHAPTER NINE 241
Find Your Voice *241*
- TRANSGENDER AND SPIRITUALITY ...241
- WOMEN AND SUPPRESSION 243
- SEX VS. GENDER 245

WOMEN, SEX, AND GENDER 246
HETROSEXUAL NORMS 247
POWER STRUCTURES 248
POVERTY: A CONTINUOUS CYCLE 249
INDIGENOUS COMMUNITIES............... 251
ASSIMILATION 252
PRIDE AND SPIRITUALITY 255
PUPPET MASTERY 258
SOCIAL MEDIA 260

CHPATER TEN 263

Be the Voice 263

PURPOSE.. 263
DEAR CANDY 265
THANK YOU MOM 267
INSPIRATION 268
WHY DON'T YOU LOVE ME? 273
PRAYER 274
SPIRITUAL AWAKENING....................... 276
THE GIFT OF LIFE 277
ALL THINGS CONNECTED.................... 278
FLOWERS THAT BLOSSOM 281
FINDING YOUR VOICE 282

BE THE VOICE. TAKE ONE STEP FURTHER 283

References 285

STRUGGLING TO BE

THE VOICE

INTRODUCTION

As each day passes, I struggle to come to terms with my new life. I find it difficult to understand and cope with all that has happened in the last few months. Firstly, losing friends in your life is not an easy experience. When you unconditionally love someone and they mislead you, it makes you question whether the friendship was genuine to begin with. As I look back on all the hurdles, the pain, and the progress, I struggle to come to terms with the present. All I see is the past. The future scares me. How can I be the voice for others when I struggle to find a voice for myself? How can I love others when I struggle to love myself and experiences that have left me broken and hurt? I truly am struggling to be the voice and am trying to cope with the last few years. Secretly, I am crying on the inside and screaming on the outside for someone to understand.

STRUGGLING TO BE THE VOICE

People might not understand what message I am intending to portray in this book but my heart is authentic and my intention to uplift others is sincere. I always say to my mother, "I see individuals for their hearts." Shouldn't we all? It feels like I have just entered an entirely new world with new emotions.

I am stuck trying to find my purpose in the world. I might not know how to write a book. I might be somewhat strange, but if I was to tell you what has happened to me throughout my life you would never believe me. All I can say for now is that it wasn't me, it was something beyond my understanding. That something showed me the way to happiness and to achieving countless openings in life. For as long as I can remember I asked God to show me all that I am or all that I could be. So as you read these pages, this is me stepping into my light. This is all that I am trying to find my voice and to speak for those of you who feel they cannot speak for themselves. As you read the pages that lie ahead, keep in mind that you are not alone in your own story, so whatever you are experiencing

STRUGGLING TO BE THE VOICE

now is essential to your spiritual growth. Let's celebrate our victories and learn from our pain and who knows what immeasurable opportunities lie ahead.

CHAPTER ONE

The Start to Every Story

FALLEN LEAVES: BEING MADE NEW

I feel as if there is a separate world inside my head. As I look out of my window and see the leaves that have fallen, they are a reminder that I am being made new. New experiences and new approaches to situations that rise in my life. Yellow leaves are my favourite at this time of the year because they remind me of my past - old and worn out; a change for something new so that new leaves can grow. The branches are still the same. The roots will always be there, but the leaves are changing making me new. As new leaves grow, I am ready to embrace the challenges that they bring.

Finding my voice in a world where it feels like I have none and where no one sees value in my words is the most challenging. I know that I am being made new. Nicholas will always know his roots and branches. My leaves are bound to change and this time they are green. They are green because they symbolize my connection to the earth as I struggle to accept my new self. I have a hard time letting my fallen leaves stay on the ground. I want to pick them up and re-attach them and hold on to old habits that no longer suit me.

THE LIGHT BEYOND THE CLOUDS

I still wait for the day where all I can see is light. The light that shines through the clouds. The light that reminds you that even when things seem blurry you have to look long and hard in the sky to see the light up and behind the clouds. I am ready to open my heart to this next chapter in my life. To see above and beyond into a life of eternal happiness and light. People might misunderstand my leaves but they will find a way to connect to my roots. My roots are the human conditions we all experience. We all have this universal condition

STRUGGLING TO BE THE VOICE

where we are subjected to trauma, tragedy, and fear that is calling us to be made new.

ILLUSION OF LIFE

Days just seem longer for some reason. Some days I wake up with no motivation, no drive, and no zest for life. I feel like giving up. I somehow find my way with God who reminds me that I am not alone. That my work here is to get clear in thought and be present in the moment. I am still heartbroken about my best friend being apart from my life I loved her. Not in a romantic way, but it was the love a brother has for a sister.

Despite this, I feel alive for the first time in years. Almost as if the universe has heard and answered my prayers. I am reminded by soft tingles on my body and a warm hug that I am enough. Even though I let my ego get in the way, I am willing to put that aside and be obedient to what I feel called to do. After all I am only

THE START TO EVERY STORY

twenty one years old having this human experience, trying to make sense of this illusion we call life.

ONENESS: WE ARE SPIRITS

We are more than our bodies, we are spirits. We are spirits created out of love and light trying to find our way back to the source of all that exists. Whether that be God, or Allah, or whomever you identify the creator as. We are unified, we are one. We are eternal beings of light in the beginning and at the end of creation. Once we begin to understand our human experiences, God seems clear and gets codified in our evolution and growth. As we grow, we can begin to understand our soul's growth on planet earth. We separate each other by race, religion, and power. But when we identify ourselves as one world, being one with everything is when we understand that God's existence is one with everything.

STRUGGLING TO BE THE VOICE

OPEN WOUNDS

Today feels a little better, I find that when I sleep I numb my pain. My words only hurt me, no one else because they make me sensitive to emotion. I am stuck trying to understand divine purpose and my life's purpose. I am confused whether God's plan for me is aligned with the plan that I have for myself. It feels like I, along with so many people, have forgotten our roots of love and light. We have forgotten who we are and are on a path of enlightenment in search for our higher selves. Far too many times we find ourselves ashamed and shunned of our human experiences that we have endured. People fail to understand that true beauty in everything stems from pain that can be mended by love. I propose that there are people just like me, who use their pain to see true beauty and the most wonderful things. We heal our own wounds through intentions of love and understanding.

If you would have asked me eight years ago if I could heal my wounds I would have thought the impossible. But I did it. God did it. He showed me that the most beautiful things we see in others is only a mirror reflecting the love we have for ourselves. We are mirroring love, hate, suffering which is driving our lives into eternal light or darkness. We are the light that exists beyond any measure. As we mirror love, love will always win because love will always reflect our intention to accept one another for our differences.

THE CALLING

How can pain feel so satisfying? I feel hurt but I feel clear in thought and driven to complete my life's purpose. It sometimes hurts to think because when I try to make sense of all that has happened I feel upset. My anger is with no one but myself. So I must trust in divine timing, in God's plan to give me the voice that I have never had. Only then can I use my words to bring love, happiness, and hopefully the greatest good to all. I envision it like this, there will be a day when you are called; all of us, to shape and to nurture those around you. There is a purpose to your life that is in alignment with God and those around you.

STRUGGLING TO BE THE VOICE

I always felt I was different. I always felt afraid. For the first time I am not. I do not know what has changed but I do know what has happened is making me new. My awakened self is understanding that we are eternal in our existence. We are powerful in our capacity to love. We are spiritual in our hearts. We are physical in our bodies. We are unified and connected in our thoughts and manifestations. When we begin to understand the self, we can begin to understand the world and what we have been called here to do.

INSPIRE

Inspire. It is the one thing that I know I was created to do. I know beyond any doubt that my soul's purpose is to see the light in others and to extend that light so that we can be the best versions of who we are destined to become.

Help me understand why in a world of so much beauty I see people who have forgotten to lead life with their hearts. They struggle to find happiness in others

THE START TO EVERY STORY

because happiness in them is non-existent. If I could spend my life understanding the human condition of suffering; a universal experience. The first place I would search is within myself. My experiences are no different than others. In fact, people have far more traumatic experiences than what I have endured. I solely want to use my voice to be the voice of many. To help them understand that they are not defined by their experiences.

YOU ARE NOT YOUR EXPERIENCES

Days like this do not feel any easier. I feel stuck as I sit here in the dark and pour my pain into these pages. I feel like I have been left stranded trying to find my way back to prosperity. How can I find strength when I feel like my life is crashing down? I tell myself that it's going to be okay. But days like this make me want to curl up in my bed and hide from the world. No matter how hard I try to break free from barriers, I am ashamed to show my face to the world. All I have ever been subjected to for most of my life is fear and judgment that results in me exemplifying my own fears to others. Trying to find the strength to move forward in my life no matter how dark things seem is my biggest obstacle to my growth. When I am strong, people find a way to knock me down. But when I am afraid is when they keep me silenced. It feels like the words to speak up are on the tip of my tongue but nothing comes out as I try to speak. I am silenced. I am speechless. All I have ever wanted is to feel like I am good enough. When the world told me I wasn't good enough was when I decided that a comfy bed was more comfortable than finding comfort from other people.

Days like this make me question how I could possibly be a light for others. I turn to God and look up at the clouds and ask, "do you love me?" On days like this, all I need is love to get me through. Without it I am left alone. I am left silenced. I need someone to pick me up and remind me that there is no shame in your experiences. You are not your experiences instead your experiences are what allow you to fall only to be reminded that someone or something will pick you up once more.

HUMAN CONDITION: UNDERSTANDING STRUGGLE

I feel like my passion to write and inspire slowly drifts away as I overthink the last few months. Much has changed and occurred leaving my perception of my life distorted. At times I am strong, but my weakness is still shown in my face. For the first time I feel safe and understood at home.

It is so easy for us to feel like we are not enough. Even after all the hurdles, and the hurt all I have is hope. I hope to see a future where we can be more inclusive, more loving, and kinder to one another. That is all I have asked of the world and when I see someone who is experiencing homelessness on the streets, or someone who is wounded because of past trauma all I can see is their hurt and sense their fears. I

STRUGGLING TO BE THE VOICE

want to understand their struggle and what experience in their life left them feeling defenceless or weak.

MIRRORING LOVE

I wish for a world where we can find the answers to human suffering is in our hearts. A world where we can all lend a hand to suffering and impoverishment. All I ask for is hope and equality to be the greatest energy that we can spread to every heart and to touch every spirit. I hope for a world where hurdles in one's life are the obstacles we overcome together. Where your pain becomes my concern and your success is the accomplishment of many. I anticipate for the day where we can put aside internal conflict and mirror love. Once we reflect kindness and compassion, we no longer judge because we understand that the light we see in the world is our light reflecting back to us. That pain we see in the world becomes confusing because we are creating it onto others as it exists in ourselves.

THE START TO EVERY STORY

Help me understand how I can make the world a better place. I feel so inclined to make a difference but I feel so much doubt. I close my eyes and envision a day where I can see change. When love is not only the force that connects us but it binds and pulls us to do the most for one another. When I am thinking it hurts because it feels as if my thoughts are not mine. When I am alone I feel scared because I feel as if there is no one to guide me. As I wake up I remind myself that I am enough. That you are enough.

DIVINE: SOMETHING GREATER

People often underestimate spirituality. They choose not to see when they choose not to believe. I'm not saying that you have to believe there is a God but consider the possibility that there might be something greater in our lives that plays a bigger role in our day-to-day life than you or I would ever know. We exist beyond the physical. We are spirits sent to each other.

STRUGGLING TO BE THE VOICE

I remember hearing in church as a little boy, "with him, in him, and through him anything is possible". So as I look beyond the clouds, I know that he is with me, with us. As I ask myself how this reality has formed, I cannot seem to understand what I cannot see. If I were to question myself, why do I exist? I know that I am a vessel merely encompassing flesh. That we are all spiritual beings. We are sent to guide and to lead each other. People might not believe, they will mislead, they will judge you for your beliefs. Don't believe in me rather believe in what your heart is telling you. Believe with your heart, see with your heart, and trust in your heart. We can manifest whatever we believe, as I believe we are co-creating the life that we have always wanted. Seeing is merely trusting with your heart and to allow all that is be made possible through faith.

OUR SPIRITUAL JOURNEY: FAITH

I struggle to be the voice because every time I speak, my words feel invalidated, my thoughts silenced.

THE START TO EVERY STORY

All I have ever dreamed, all I have wanted is to feel like I was valuable to others. To feel as if my voice mattered even if the world struggled to hear me. I dig myself in my thoughts deeper and deeper leaving me feeling conflicted. I always underestimate myself, I constantly feel like I am not enough. We need to show people how we can heal the hearts of many through the intention of love. My heart aches when I see how people are so quick to judge me and falsify their judgments based on perceptions or rumours of me. I have begged God for too long that one day I might have the voice that I have never had. I have stayed silent for too long. I have stayed still. Even if the results of what I anticipate doing end up failing, my heart will show in all I do. Struggle is inevitably a human experience but faith is our spiritual journey reminding us who we are as we experience life through human conditions we are subjected to.

CHAPTER TWO

We Are One

LABELS: FREE YOUSELF

My mother is my greatest influencer in life because she has reminded me that I am liberated from all worries, free from my trauma, and free from my suffering that has kept me rooted in pain. She has given me a chance to be heard as I screamed out for help, changing my whispers into words and my mumbles into progress. So I want you to liberate yourself from any human condition that has kept you down for too long. Be free from any label. Be free from trauma that has left you stuck or broken because you are not labeled by your experiences. Your experiences are merely there to mold you into the person who you were always destined to be.

WE ARE ONE

PIECES OF ME: MISSING

As I look back at the last few years, I am reminded about how I used to dream that others would notice me in the hallways. I wanted others to define how valuable I could be when I struggled to love myself. There were pieces of me missing because I allowed myself to get lost. I was so lost that I couldn't find who I was. Now I am no longer afraid to hide the real me. I can reflect, remember, and learn from my life. I have learned that to be strong we must confront our weaknesses. There are times when we are lost, times where we hide ourselves because we fear judgment. When I feel like I am surrounded by darkness, I look towards others for inspiration and guidance. The voice inside my head tells me that I can be unstoppable once I allow myself to do the impossible through faith. Pieces of me may be lost, but they will always be found. You will never understand how it feels like to be constantly in the dark until you have been there. Like your thoughts and feelings do not matter. But if you do know you also understand that

STRUGGLING TO BE THE VOICE

there is no way to suppress the real you. You will rise and succeed once you begin to realize that no matter where you are currently in your life, you are continuously reminded to look towards the light.

INNER VOICE

Do you ever get a gut feeling about someone or a premise about what is about to happen? You have this senseless thought that appears in your head maybe in a picture or words, and moments later you have this knowing of what is about to happen or what you should do next. Most of us disregard these feelings because we assume that it is just a coincidence. However it is your gut feeling, your inner voice guiding you.

Let that inner voice guide you and with it you will be successful in all you do. Allow yourself to fight the darkness in the world so that all you can see is light. It is so easy to say "trust that inner voice" when you are at a point where in life where it feels you have little to believe in. No matter how small your belief is, it is powerful beyond any measure because it can change hearts, touch lives, and let you achieve countless opportunities that are yet to be discovered by you. Your heart is the greatest weapon you have against the darkness that life throws at you.

SOCIAL CONDITIONING: THE AUTHENTIC YOU

As things are starting to turn around, I cannot help but reflect on my past. As much as these writings are therapeutic for me, within this text are held a lot of secrets, a lot of hurt that I have kept bottled inside for years. This book has given me the chance to express myself in a healthy way. I am slowly getting to this place where I feel more comfortable in leading and directing my life positively. I cannot help but remember the summers spent locked in my room as I stared out of my window praying for a day where I could escape from my city. I wanted to find my place in the world and most importantly, find my voice. You see, I was just like you as I cried for help and longed for someone to hear me. The thing is, no matter how hard I tried to

STRUGGLING TO BE THE VOICE

scream it seems like no one was able to hear me. Every time I endured relationship struggles, or problems with self-confidence, self-love, I had to learn how to love myself for not being anyone else but the person who I was created to become. I was on this journey of understanding myself and the struggles I encountered allowed me to feel more comfortable to express all aspects of myself without judgment because I feared judgment. I feared the way people saw me because I grew up in a world where they conditioned me to believe that opinions matter. That the way I saw myself was not as important as the way others saw me. It caused me to fold my jeans, and wear clothes that appealed to others and had no connection to me. I was trying to become someone I thought I should be, but was not. As we are constantly changing and evolving, do not put aside your authentic you because you can hide behind your clothes but you cannot hide behind your truest and most accurate representation of you.

WE ARE ONE

ETERNAL BEINGS

We are eternal beings beyond any measure. I understand this because I know that there is something beyond any theory, beyond any dream that is pushing me towards the path that I have been called to pursue. I know that in my darkest times I will find strength of something greater. I know that my story is just a story and not the conclusion to how I choose to end my chapters. I know that beyond any measure I am co-creating the life that I was destined to live and the path that I was struggling to follow. In my weakness, I know that there is power because my pain is the power that drives me to purpose. If I have given up then I have not trusted that the power which is steering my life in the right direction is accurate. Any of us can plan our own lives but God will plan it best. In all that you do, remember that you are carrying a heart that reminds you to act on love. So follow it. Remember that the person they expect you to be and who you truly are is beyond imagination. The essence of your existence is divinely and there is no accident in the creation of you.

STRUGGLING TO BE THE VOICE

So when you feel like giving up on life's ways of challenging you, accept it. Accept that not every challenge is challengeable and not every obstacle you will overcome. We are co-creating the life that has been and will always be God's plan. In all that you are the root of who you truly are is your heart. It is your heart that speaks to many, it changes lives. God reads your heart. God speaks to your heart. Knowing this, see not with your eyes rather see with your heart. I have always loved hearts because they give us the power to heal and to hold that force which is divinely.

UNIQUENESS

I woke up today feeling happy and confused. Happy because I feel like I am starting to understand the reasons as to why I am here on earth. Reasons like why do I exist alongside you? And why we all are sharing this experience. That leads to more questions when we question what reality is. I am confused because there are more questions to this life than there are answers. We all ask ourselves where do we come from but we don't really challenge ourselves to explore the possibilities. I am trying to reach this place of enlightenment where all questions can begin to surface as answers instead of questions. I believe we are lost only to be reminded that as long as we remain lost we will always be followed. We are never really alone. You are never alone. So I plead with you to remind yourself that when life turns dark and situations arise, you are lost only to be guided and surely to be followed. You can never fully find yourself until you are willing to search for the things that make you feel whole once again. Many of us are on this path of trying to uncover who we truly are. Yet the person who we truly are is there, it is just waiting to surface only to remind ourselves of why we are unique. You are unique because there is no other you. Just like how two snowflakes can never truly match, you can never walk or smile or laugh just like anyone other than you.

We are all lost, we are all unique. So yes, you may be confused as to why these experiences exist. Why we must fall and cry to heal or why we must jump and dance to be free? Your soul is changing, you are evolving to reach higher states of consciousness that you could never imagine. Your journey is not to uncover who you could be but to unleash the real you so that you can be the truest, best version of yourself that you are seen as but not recognized as. You are created to understand that as much as this is a human experience we have chosen to partake in, it is a spiritual warfare that we are trying to understand within ourselves.

I have started to understand that no matter how hard we try to persevere in what we think may be our purpose, is not always the path we must take. We are always being shown by the universe the answers of where to go next through signs such as numerology or conversations that strike feelings that resonate with us deeply. I have searched for too long trying to make sense of life and my purpose here. Most of us say we feel different and that is because we are. We are different so that we can encounter experiences with each other that are significant to our spiritual growth

WE ARE ONE

and journey. If we were all alike in personality, the spiritual growth we would experience would be little to none because everyone would be alike and everyone would have the same perspective about life. Our differences push us to differentiate from one another; as a result, we are not only growing spiritually but humanity is changing continuously.

POSITIVE CHANGE SIGNIFIES GROWTH

I have found that staying silent in a world that suppresses' opinion is not a solution. So I challenge you to use your voice as a way to make change in your experiences and your encounters. I have not always been understood, simply because my philosophy in life is that we are on the earth to discover the heart of who we truly are. We are blinded by illusion, we are restricted by circumstance. You have the power now and forever to make a difference. To do the things you love, to share moments with the people who make you want to treasure them. Allow yourself to find out who you are by discovering who you were created to become. You will begin to find your place in the world once you understand how you are connected to all things. I wish I could have learned this lesson years ago but I was trying to uncover a part of me that only mirrored what was shown to me by the rest of society. Take your life and steer your journey to encounter every obstacle as a chance to do better. Because when you are at your lowest is when you become the strongest. You can be all that you were meant to be once you uncover your heart. It all starts with you. It is you, because God reads your heart.

SPEAK YOUR TRUTH

I looked outside my window this morning and saw the first drops of snow this year. It is a reminder from God that there is a new me emerging. As I pour my words onto these pages, I want people to discover who they are in the process of learning that we are all sharing this human experience. When I was younger, I prayed almost every day. I prayed and prayed that God would bring a day where I could break away from everyone around me and everything I had known. I wanted to get lost so that maybe I could find myself through the process. I hated the fact that when I looked at myself all I saw was someone who was unhappy with himself. Someone who was trying to fit in with what society was.

When I tried to be me, they told me I was wrong for it. They told me I should not laugh too loud before people would call me gay. They said not to express myself through gestures such as hugging because that was not an appropriate form of showing love for a male. They said I had a learning disability and a comprehension problem because I didn't like the material they presented to me at school. So I set out years later, now, trying to explore my creativity. That boy was six. That person was me. I struggled to be the voice and every time they said I couldn't, my mother told me I could. Let me take you on a journey to explore my story and maybe just perhaps you might get a glimpse of how to be a better parent, friend, or see the heartache of how a lost boy struggled to find himself.

STRUGGLING TO BE THE VOICE

Let me tell you a story about how my voice never became acknowledged until I finally spoke my truth.

CONFLICTED

As I write these pages, I am conflicted whether I should continue. Bringing up old memories is too painful to remember. I wish that life could be a lot easier so that we all could have the ideal human experience. I share these pages that follow in the hope to direct your life so that you can become exactly who you want to be. I am stuck in my head trying to unravel all that there is about me. People might critique me and say that this book is meaningless. But it is my story. It is our story. It is the story of how we tried to get back up and were knocked down no matter how hard we tried. It's the story that is going to teach us all, including me, how we can discover who we are by breaking away from a society that restricts us. So I think to myself how can I make a change? How can I give you a voice? I am only one person and maybe my voice is insignificant to those who have much more power and money, but my voice matters. Your voice matters. Struggling to be the voice is that voice that we have all struggled to be. Whether it was at six or now in our life it's our story where we learn to take our power back.

Even if these pages seem insignificant, that might be true, but this story exists in the hope to liberate all of us from whatever we are currently going through. When I was six the world did not seem fair or just. As I am twenty one I see the same story. How can we do better and how can we drive our life with purpose and passion? Discover who you are as you dig deep into your fears and traumas. Let's face them together; let's speak the words that you know but have been afraid to express, and maybe together we can try to understand why we really are here.

REFLECTIONS

It's hard to remember moments in your life that you tried so hard to forget. I tried to forget how I was bullied or physically abused many times. It is too painful to remind myself of all that has happened when I am trying to move forward. I went from being a victim to a survivor but it took me years to get there. I never wanted to play the victim but the reality was that at one point, I was. It was so conflicting as a child to go to church and they would deliver a message of how to be kind to one another or "treat others the way you want to be treated" they said. Despite this, when I went to school all I felt was darkness around me. When you are bullied the world feels different, colors seem less vibrant, family feels less important, love seems like it is always lacking no matter how many people try to bring you back up. I felt like my creativity and passion was lost in an institution that manipulated and conditioned me what to think rather than how to think. I was depressed because I didn't like the way we learned and I didn't like being away from my family during school hours. But they made me believe that it was normal to feel isolated or scared. So I did what most of us do, I followed the structure of the educational system and learned to have good church values.

WE ARE ONE

What I realized much later in life was that my self-esteem was based on a grade and my future in academia was in the hands of people who would tell me whether or not I had the capability. So I suppressed my emotion because in school you do not have time to feel anything. I swallowed my words because my voice did not matter, the voice of the authority figures like the teachers or the principals did. In listening to everyone else but me I lost myself. I forgot the stories my mom used to tell me on the little brown couch in our basement. I forgot the memories of me and my mom dancing in the kitchen on a Saturday morning singing "two times three equals six and three times six is eight-tee-eeen". I was losing myself in order to fit in. There was no love or passion in school and I found myself living a false reality with false hopes and dreams. When you are younger they ask you what you want to be. We say crazy things like an astronaut. Here I was, as an adult, being told that who I would become was in the hands of someone telling me whether or not I would be successful in life.

STRUGGLING TO BE THE VOICE

QUICK TO JUDGE

They were so quick to judge me. Before I could read, they diagnosed me with a learning disability. The sad thing is that I believed them. But because my mother believed otherwise she knew that their opinion of me was only their opinion. She saw not with her eyes but with her heart. So we ran to the nearest library in Streetsville, Ontario near our house and we read my favorite book that made me feel safe. It was called Nicholas at the Library by Hazel Hutchings. So on a cold Friday afternoon, I would run home from school and we would go in our red GMC and explore the mysteries in the library. What I learned from that book is that every trip to the library was an adventure. It wasn't so much that the books were the exciting part, it was the stories that allowed me to escape reality for a second. Every Friday it became a routine that I would check out any book in my grade one class. What I didn't know was that one day, I would complete my own chapters in my own story of life that would take me to a place of solitude. Those childhood stories are the child parts of me trying to be understood and every so often I would revisit them as my truth in life.

I learned early on in life that many of us are aware of what is happening yet we do not use our voice to make choices to change. So I will use my voice to be the voice of those who matter. For the ones who have experienced neglect or abuse. You are not alone, I too have experienced this. For the people who have been labeled or outcasted, I too have been subjected to this. At six, I understood that my struggles were everyday struggles of many others and I was not the only one experiencing this. So I knew that I could be strong for others who did not know how to be.

LOVE AND SUPPORT

I remember another boy at my school who was double my size; he tried to push my sister onto the concrete floor. I remember standing in the way holding the space between my sister and that boy, this would keep her safe. He pushed me numerous times and every time he pushed me down I remember standing back up to hold that space. I refused for this to be the story that would define her later in life. So when I witnessed bullying, anger, and hatred I knew that it arose from a place much deeper in people. It arises from their deeper core that feels the most vulnerable and weak at a time when seemingly, their power has been taken away. This became not only my story but every story of the people whose hearts I touched and who touched mine and who weren't able to speak against injustice. The fact that someone would receive pleasure from inflicting pain onto someone made me question why I went to church and learned about love and why at school, kids showed me another way of being. This experience made me question how much the world needed to stand and hold the space for love and support.

CHAPTER THREE

All That I Am

I WILL NOT HURT MY ENEMY

I am stuck trying to understand why my purpose feels lost in doing things that feel pointless. I never dreamed that the life I could envision would be here, in school. School brings memories of pain because I often have to revisit my childhood memories.

I had a dream today. I dreamed that I was physically fighting with some of the people from my past who hurt me. For a second, it felt good and I was winning. What I now realize is that I never want to be that person who seeks pleasure from someone else's pain. I don't want to be that boy that smiled every time he tried to push my sister onto the concrete floor. So I search for a medium between forgiveness and my pain. All I know is that I struggled to stay strong to stand in the light when I chose to fight back. I am no different than my enemy once I use their weapons against them. In fact, I just become a mirror, imitating them and carrying out inexcusable behavior patterns.

So do I live with trauma or do I transform trauma into bliss? Every time I try to be happy someone tries to find a way to disrupt my happiness. So I get back up to fight a disagreement, not a war. I will not use my enemies' weapons instead I need no weapon because I must think of all the people who are left weeping and abandoned. Teach me to be strong and to stand for what is just. Teach me to stand in the light so that others may too. Show me how to do better so that I can show others and maybe there is a lesson to be learned.

PERFORMITIVITY: HANDS IN THE POCKET

So I was silenced. My words didn't matter. My speech was impaired. When I tried to ask for help they blamed me. They said "It is your fault". I learned at the age of six that when you ask for help it is not there. The school blames you for not fitting in with your classmates. Your parents blame you for not being like everyone else and the church tries to understand but might not understand the struggles of a six-year-old boy. How do you explain to someone that you are trying to co-exist in a world where there really are no people like you? I used to turn on the television and see people who would make a difference in people's lives. Whether that be through counseling or philanthropy. All I had ever wanted was to be like these people. What I realized much later in life was that it was much easier being myself since I did not have to try to be anyone else. That who I was, felt like it was enough because I did not know another way of being. I questioned existence because I saw all these people trying to be someone else they did not understand. I wanted to feel and be myself; but every time I laughed they called me gay.

When I tried to speak they told me to seal my lips because my voice would crack. So I did what my mother told me. I did what most mothers would want their sons to do. I walked with my hands in my pockets and kept my posture straight. I did it so much that I would practice it. I tried to perfect it so that I could pass in the classroom and in my home. I tried to talk less because kids at school said, "boys don't talk that much". I would turn my smile into a frown because boys are not supposed to be happy. Boys are supposed to be serious. Everything I had known about the world around me felt corrupted. Yet everyone made me feel like my perception of the world was wrong.

So I learned how to perform at an early age and I got so good at it that I knew how to fake a smile or a laugh on cue. My emotions and persona became deceitful and I was trapped in my mind because I lived in secret, I lived the biggest lie inside my head not being who I felt I truly was. Every time my grandparents said I acted like a girl, I knew I would be in trouble. Every time the other children would tell my siblings that they thought I was gay, goosebumps would shiver down my spine. Every time I was too nice, I knew I was in trouble for not performing correctly. So I associated fear with being myself. It wasn't me who created that but it was the people around me telling me that the essence of who I was, was not enough. My grandparents never saw it as love. So I was conflicted with who I was in a closet that never really existed. People confused love with a sexual orientation by using words like gay or fag; words that I didn't even know what they meant until years later.

PEBBLES ON THE GROUND

Recess was my favorite time at school because that was when I would wait to sit by myself against the walls of the school and play with pebbles on the ground. The pebbles on the ground reminded me that being alone wasn't always a bad thing because it gave me time to reflect on who I was. Pebbles felt cold and dark but heavy, much like what I was feeling on the inside. To try to cut the pebbles open and see what's on the inside you would see the heavy weight that it carries and all the layers that have solidified in the pebble. I didn't know at that point in my life that the pebble was symbolic to what I was going through at that time in my life.

ALL THAT I AM

Throughout elementary, I struggled to find friends to play with on the playground. On a good day, I would find more than twelve pebbles and to me that was a sign that maybe one day things would be better. As I would play with the pebbles I remember trying to understand why other children would laugh and play and yet there I was trying to understand why I didn't fit in. Was their happiness real or was it a lie that we told ourselves to feel more inclusive? As many of my schoolmates would walk past me, I felt invisible. They didn't ask me to play with them because maybe they could never possibly understand what it felt like to be alone or afraid or even misunderstood until it occurred in their own life.

YOUR TEARS NEVER FALL

I felt scared every time my grandfather beat me down physically and I chose to get back up. I remember he would form two fists and point them in my face to taunt me about the beating he was about to give me. I was afraid because every time I had to do class presentations, my arms would shake and my voice would crack and the other kids at school would laugh. I tried not to smile too much because if I was happy my grandfather would beat me or the kids at school would call me gay. I tried to understand how much I loved to smile. I think it is the way to show kindness that makes us feel like our existence here is validated. Our smiles let us know that whatever we're going through will be okay someday.

In my trials and in my fears I found solitude when I was alone. I found purpose in the stories my mother told me and in the authenticity I saw in others. I wanted to speak to touch hearts, not to destroy them. So every time my grandfather told me I was stupid, I forgave him because he did not know better. Every time he threw me down the stairs and stepped on the back of my neck, I forgave him because his actions were just actions not intention. Every time he twisted my ears and told me I was gay or slow, I knew that he simply did not know better. I remembered what my mother told me in the stories we used to read. That the stories were my story, our story. How we choose to fill our pages is up to us.

In church, I would touch my heart and I would sing 'Children of the light'. I loved that song because it reminded me that no matter how dark life may be the light that we are searching for is us. If you ever find yourself lost in the darkness turn to the light of God. Turn to the light of the world. Forgive. You might not always forget but get the lesson and move forward. No matter how many times my grandfather hurt me, I still tried to find it in my heart to forgive him. Forgive, because for you to get happiness in life you must give love. My mother once told me, "Your tears never really fall because God is always there to lift them back up." If that is true then you should never worry if abuse or trauma has left you feeling powerless. If I had that faith much earlier in life, it would have allowed me to move forward instead of being stuck in my story. Something I think we all forget at times.

STRUGGLING TO BE THE VOICE
RUNNING AWAY FROM FEAR

I did not understand forgiveness because I could not fathom how people carried pain and acted against others with hatred. I hope that I do not mirror hate or show people that fitting in is the way we need to feel understood. So I will try not to perform to fit in. I will smile to give others hope, the hope that I wish for everyone to see in the world. You cannot understand fear until you are left vulnerable or abandoned. Fear makes us turn to war with each other because we are afraid of being hurt. So, we either run away from fear or confront it with weapons or anger because no one has ever taught us how to cope with fear. It seems that somehow the biggest war we end up fighting is with each other, because we choose to hate and we choose to separate ourselves from one another instead of

coming together. Life never intended for us to feel lost, but we get lost in the ways of the world and the weight of responsibility given to us.

They said, "You're six and you're a big boy and are old enough to be mature." So we never have time to think, grow, or change. We end up lost in the weight of the world and consumed by others when we watch the way people live their lives. We watch people on social media and follow them on Instagram. We try new looks and new clothes forever changing, always adapting. Trying to be made new, because who you see in the mirror is not who you intended to be. It does not feel like the you who wants to wake up and smile at yourself. We get lost in our mind, lost in the world. The result is that we grow up feeling lost, never having a chance to discover who we are because the weight of the world gets heavier. Our responsibilities increase, our lives are always changing. We never get stuck in the moment because time is not still. We never get a chance to feel alive because we have never lived for ourselves. When you are in your mind, you will always exist there but once you leave your mind, the world seems brighter and you stop feeling lost but instead found.

No matter how many times you feel incomplete or less than, know that there is something greater than you that holds the image of your destiny. Struggling to

STRUGGLING TO BE THE VOICE

be the voice is not just my story, it's our story of how we tried and got back up. It's the story of no matter how dark things seem there was always a way to pick ourselves back up. You might feel incomplete in your life now, only for experiences later in your life to teach you and fulfil the parts of you that felt incomplete. You will be tested, you will be pushed but it is to make you into the person who you were meant to be. Never give up. Never stop believing because what cannot seem possible is that which is possible. All is possible. All can be achieved. Listen to your heart, follow it and believe because they will tell you that you are a fool to question or to redirect your path to where your happiness will be.

You are challenging the fears that you have ran away from. You are confronting your past that you neglected and are pushing yourself to be the self that only you could dream of. When your dreams become fantasies that turn into reality was when you allowed yourself to feel in the moment and to trust that the universe holds the answers you seek. In all that you are, you are trying to unravel the parts of you that are conflicted. Your place of worship holds the foundation on which you stand. Your kindness holds the key to every heart. Every heart you will touch is the touch that causes change because how you affect others is the greatest affect the world needs. Today, allow yourself to be the key to every mystery you dared not to solve. Speak for those who have been lost in injustice and conflicted in their actions.

Remember this, the life you are living is not yours. Only because it is lent to you, this body is lent to you to use it to move in the direction of your purpose. You are the vessel encompassing flesh that is being steered and directed constantly. Nobody said it was going to be easy but the easiest lesson is the one that you forgot that when life seems tough, don't give up; you are equipped with just enough to handle life's obstacles. You are given a brain to help you think logically and a heart to help you remember why you came here. If that is what you are given, it is because God believed it was enough for you to do whatever task you came here to accomplish.

STRUGGLING TO BE THE VOICE

TRUST YOUR HEART

One thing that I know for certain is that you only get knocked down to try again. That sometimes the answers you seek are not always the answers you need. When you are in alignment with what you need to do, you will know. The right people will come in and help you, things will be aligned down to the last second. Someone will tutor you and explain to you all the concepts you need to know for your test. You will encounter someone who will offer you a job or walk you to show you where you can find the library. Remember that no two paths cross if they are not meant to. You will know because you will only feel joy and happiness. That does not always mean that where you are right now is where you will always be. It just emphasizes that when you are on the path that God wants you to be on, you will know.

When the answers that are missing from our life are nowhere to be found, turn to God. You do not know who you really are, all you know is that you have been placed here on the earth and you are here to try to understand why. You do not know who you are because you are more than just 'you' who has existed throughout this life. All you know is that you are from something beyond our imagination, something greater. So when you feel down or life knocks you astray, all you can do is turn to that which is greater than you. That energy speaks back because it either directs or redirects us to be on the path it wants us to be on. You do not have the answers to why we are sharing this human experience together. I do not have all the answers to why we are here. But what your mind is telling you is to figure out how to blend in, how to survive, how to find a good job and make money. Your heart tells you one thing, and that is to trust. It is the only thing you can do to every problem the mind has to offer. So when you are on the verge of crisis or have lost someone know that there is no other way but the way that God speaks to us. We are all learning to be braver and stronger than ever before but we are being pushed and tested to get there.

STRUGGLING TO BE THE VOICE

A BEACON OF LIGHT

My mother said something that encouraged me to move towards my destiny. She said to me that this chapter of my life is just a chapter of my story. A story that shows people that we have no control. We have no control in the circumstances that we are subjected to. We have no control in the outcome of our lives but what we do have control over is how we use our stories to help shape a better world. One of the hardest things for me to do is to close a chapter that I never thought would happen. Walking away from school and from an environment where I touched many hearts is one of the hardest journeys for me. After speaking to numerous professors, students, and many others I felt that if I never pursued my calling that time might not ever come again. So I am doing only what I feel is right and moving forward. I am taking a chance to follow my heart into places I could not ever dream of. The other day, as I was walking back from my class I ran into one of my students in the parking lot. She said, "Thank you." I asked her why and she said, "Thank you for making a difference in my life, and one day you will make a difference in someone else's life."

For as long as I can remember, all I wanted to be was a light for others. She reminded me that I have, we have a light in all of us that we are searching for. I ask God to lead me to the highest good that I can be. To help me lead a life that is purposeful and full of hope. As a child, I never knew that dreams could manifest into reality. That the stories we heard from others could one day lead to stories of our own. That the life we live is not ours but it is for us to use in service for each other. To make an impact. To ignite a spark. To remind ourselves and each other that the imprint we leave on the world is the impact we have on the lives we touch. Remember this, living our life to the highest good, to living our life to impact and to start a chain reaction in the world that is the story you leave behind when you pass from here. Because the people who do not know about you when you are alive will always remember your story as the legacy you left behind so that one day that story can be retold and transformed to remind others that you lived the best life you could. A life that was authentic, flawed, and joyful. A life that showed we did not know how best to fit in but we knew that by being ourselves was enough to live our life the way we wanted to. In my chapters that have left me feeling misunderstood, I know that I can understand why I had to stand in the light to help others see the best in me. They might not have understood me but I know now that it really is okay to just be. To be 'you' that is authentic, that is misunderstood because that is your light. This life was never meant to be misaligned with our passions. It is only that we failed to lead a life of bliss and instead, choose to do things that couldn't make us happy.

WHY ARE WE HERE?

Why are we here? What is the purpose of this human experience? It is a question that we all ask ourselves but never reflect on enough. I understand it like this. That knowing you are equipped with just enough to build the life you want. It is not an accident that we are all existing as I speak. That the people who are passing into our lives come into our lives for a day or maybe a year. That the people who are just passing by in our lives teach us something new that we did not know before. They teach us to be kinder, loving and how to be better overall. Whether we have learned one lesson or more, each encounter is no accident.

Every lesson is just a lesson and it is meant to move us towards our destiny that we are co-creating with the Divine. It is no accident that you are pushing yourself into being more positive. You are exactly where you need to be to help shape a better character. The truth is you are moving through life faster and stronger as you learn to make better choices, to trust, and to hold onto your faith in knowing that everything will be okay. In knowing this, you start to see that your pain is your progress to a better you. We are not meant to have all the answers to life's biggest questions such as why are we here. Instead, we are given all we need and have answers to exactly what we need to move through this life. Step into your destiny, walk out of your comfort zone. Do things that you could never imagine yourself doing. Live the life you have always thought of but have been too afraid to explore. Utilize and experience this human journey and look at ever experience as a lesson to enhance your spiritual growth. Connect yourself to the energy that is in everything, in everyone. Know that we are all connected somehow, it is the energy that flows through everyone. The energy that allows every heart to beat and every walk to walk another mile. It is the energy in a hug or a hello. It binds and unifies us connecting us through this human experience. Understanding that this energy that connects us all fears no race, no religion, it is universal. It is moving in and out of us and our lives knowingly and unknowingly. It wants us to trust ourselves, to use our stories to help others so that we do not become defined by our stories.

I stand before you to liberate every burden, to free you from the tragedy you allowed to define you. For those who find themselves trapped in the space of an experience, I am here to remind you, it really is okay to not feel okay with circumstances that have made you feel stuck. Do not allow others to distinguish your light because God has promised that "In him there is no darkness, in him there is only light". So when you feel like life takes a toll on your health and the path that you are walking has not shown its rewards, trust that God is moving you into alignment with him and to where you need to be.

We are all trying to find our way back to the source. We are just searching for a way to get there. Whether that be through prayer, meditation, or through trauma. We are trying to understand our human experiences and what it is that connects us all to each other. What is it within us besides that light that we wish to see in the world? God speaks to those who listen. So when you are upset or angry because you lost your job, God is speaking to your heart because he can see the whole picture when you cannot. So you find out a few years later if you would have stayed in that job you might not be happy. Our prayers, our voice in our head tells us to trust because it is the greatest skill we have. Let things be the way they are. To listen and trust is to just be in the present moment and accept whatever is to come. So when you are alone and confused and you pray every time you touch your heart, there is some peace in knowing that you do not walk this journey alone. Every time you hear that whisper that speaks to your heart, you are reminded that you are loved because if you do not believe that there is something greater than you then you are alone in this universe trying to understand why you are here. You will live a life that you did not intend to live. You will be disappointed because your prayers are non-existent. You will forget how to find your way back to the source of all that is. You will be stuck trying to understand your human experience rather than your spiritual one that comes through human experiences. You will walk through life losing trust, not understanding what it is that connects us. To lose sight of God is to live our life blindly, half asleep, never knowing what happens next, never believing and trusting. To trust God is to believe that there is something greater than you that you never would know could be possible without believing in God.

ALL THAT I AM

VALIDATION, AUTHENTICTY, AND KINDNESS

I have searched through life trying to understand experiences by dwelling on them. What I realized is that every time I was knocked down only to get back up once more to try again. Every time someone told me I was not smart enough, it was only so that I would work harder to show myself that I was smart enough. The validation I was searching for did not have to come from other people because it started with me. Once I validated the things I did not like about myself, I became wise because I was able to leave my insecurities in my experience. I learned to just be myself so that I live for myself. As long as I loved who I was, other people would love me for who I was because they would see that authenticity in me. I wanted to show others how to live a life that is filled with abundance and joy. So be happy and grateful that you are here to use your voice and make a mark on the world with every life you will inspire.

Search for the answers of the universe within your spirituality or spiritual belief. Know that your spirit can never fully be free until you escape from every social condition that has kept you silenced. When you are in the space of your mind and your mind tells you to live but your heart tells you to give and forgive, that is how to live. Turn to the person next to you and ask how you can be all you can in this life and utilize this life to be of service for others so that when you leave from here you and I know you have accomplished your soul's purpose here. A life worth living is a life that allows you to feel fulfilled in the acts of kindness that you do. For example if you open the door for someone and they say thank you, there is a spark that goes off in you. It is this spark that makes you feel rewarded for what you have done. It reminds you that your actions are in alignment with why you are here, to love.

See rather with your heart instead of your eyes because your heart sees the best in every situation and in everyone. Your eyes tend to judge and God does not judge. We all want to feel loved and connected to one another. We all want to feel accepted. We want to feel noticed but the sad part about this is that people do not notice you when you're alive, they notice you when

ALL THAT I AM

you're gone. They notice the number of times you smiled or laughed or how you treated other people. They remember your kindness. Simple acts of kindness remind us that our purpose in life is to be made whole. Being whole means being one with God and one with each other. Your heart is the greatest compass you have because it leads you to show kindness and compassion for the simple things that life offers. Let this be a reminder to you that love is the greatest gift you can give. Not only is love the greatest gift but it is an even greater gift when you receive.

CHAPTER FOUR

Voiceless

HE WAS AFRAID

I was six, I lived in a basement. I saw the world much differently than the way people presented it to me. There was this brown couch my mother would lie on, and as I laid next to her she used to tell me stories and read to me. I used to dream that I could be in the stories she told me or that one day my family could overcome our economic status. At school they called me poor, they said "You live in a basement". But I watched my mom wake up every day at three in the morning and never miss a day of work so that one day I could have a story of my own that would have less struggle and more happiness. I used to sleep in the top bunk with my sister on the bottom and I would pray that we might not have to struggle one day. I used to be afraid. But life has made me conquer all my experiences.

VOICELESS

I had this idea called happy days where I would place glow-in-the-dark stickers onto my bed every time a day passed with some kind of memorable moment. I would watch the stickers glow in the dark as I prayed. I remember at the age of six, I learned that light will always shine no matter how dim things seem, sometimes you just have to look long and hard to see the light. So I applied the same reasoning with people. I knew there was a light in everyone, I just had to look deep. I saw that light in my mother because some nights when I was afraid and I cuddled in her bed with my father, I would hold onto her hair.

When mommy used to wake up at three in the morning, I had my eyes wide awake as I felt the tug of her hair as she awoke. I used to jump out of bed and help her get ready for work. "Here's your juice mommy, for work," I would say. For most people, they might be able to resonate with seeing their parents working hard so that their life can be better. She used to tuck me back to sleep and kiss me on the cheek. Another day, another school day that I would one day share with you.

STRUGGLING TO BE THE VOICE

That six-year-old was afraid. Always picked last during gym class. He sat at the back of the class. When he had to do class presentations, he would curl up and hide. He was afraid and ashamed that people would judge him. He learned at a very young age that the world can be cruel, because people will judge you and label you and tell you that you need to change to fit in. What I never understood was how come we all are unique yet we are told to be the same to fit in. I never understood why even as a child the world could view you as a monster.

MONSTER: CONFORM PLEASE

I used to hug the other children on the playground when they felt unhappy. All I knew was love, all most children know is innocence, and all I wanted to be was kind. But they told me I was wrong. The teacher had told my parents that my actions were touchy and because of this I was given the label of being inappropriate. She said to my mother, "When he gets older and hugs other people they will not like that."

VOICELESS

That is probably true but maybe if we received more affirmations of love we would be in a more peaceful world. How do you wake up one day and despite who you are, forget that, so you adapt a new persona to please other people. We are teaching children how to be children and because of this, they can never fully discover who they are and grow up into the person they want to be. When we condition them from a young age what to know and how to think in their adult years, they feel lost because they could never safely be who they are, and because we are afraid of how the world views us we take on new personas trying to find the one that best fits us, that best pleases society. We are judging each other without even realizing it and because of this, no one feels safe being who they are because we fear judgment more than we fear being who we really are.

A BROKEN HEART

When someone says to you "I love you" the real question is, do you really mean what you say. They say broken bones are supposed to hurt more than spoken words but I disagree because your word is your whisper. When you use your words to heal and to love, people recognize that. So when you say, I love you and you truly mean it, your whisper, the other person feels is that you are truthful. But when you say, I love you and hidden behind those words, is a feeling of deceit or dishonesty, the other person hears a whisper hinting dishonesty. This leads to a broken heart because from the start of the words "I love you", it was clear that "I" is sometimes the reason we do not consider how we make other people feel. When your intention is to do good, God sees that. When your intention is to be dishonest or to inflict pain, it is the deadliest weapon you can use to hurt someone; and even something like "I love you" leads to a broken heart. There is a lack of love in our world because so many of us have been lied to or have been led by dishonesty. Every time we were told "I love you" and our mother, brother, father, or whoever did not mean it, their words became their weapon and all we were left with was a broken heart. So every time you say "I love you", say it from your heart so that it is no longer a weapon but instead an affirmation. Love is infinite and there is no quantity or price that can describe that infinite force. Let your words be your bond and your commitment so that broken hearts can be mended and the pain and hurt that we see in others can be mended by love.

FOLLOW YOUR HEART

Sometimes I wish I wasn't myself because being me feels like being an outlier from so many people. I wish I was popular or would get high marks in school. I know I serve a purpose in life, just sometimes I wish I knew what it was. Maybe I could be that kid on all the sports teams or the one who has a rewarding job. My mom tells me to be more social but in doing so, I feel like nothing, almost invisible. I feel like I can never really be myself without someone judging me or criticizing my character. We all want to be ourselves in a world that is based so much on appearance. If you have a tattoo in the wrong spot, you can't get the job you want or if you play too many sports and are doing poorly in academics, you won't go far in your achievements in academia. How can you truly be yourself with that being enough to get the job of your choice and the grades that you desire? The truth is that in a society that is focused on social conditioning, you cannot be yourself without judgment but be yourself anyways. There is a light in you that shines brighter than anything I have ever seen, so when you are the girl who rocks pink hair with tattoos, I see character. While others will judge you for it, know that there is no other person you can be because they have already been taken by someone else; the only person you are left to be is you. Follow your heart even if people around you might not agree with you for it. If you believe that people of color, LGBTQ+, or women face discrimination and are oppressed, stand with them. We need to start to give all communities of oppression, the voice they have never had. If you are aware that certain communities face adversity and you are not taking diligent steps to confront the problem, then you are silent and your voice no longer becomes heard. Speak for those who cannot speak for themselves. This is how you follow your heart and who knows maybe in doing so you help to pave a brighter future for someone else.

LOST ON THE NEVER ENDING BRIDGE

Life takes us to unexpected places, sometimes even when we don't expect to end up there. Life is a wonder, a journey, and what we call an experience. We choose what path we take in life and we learn to excel and grow individually. People come into our life to teach us at least one lesson, and so we get the lesson and move forward. New friends, new school, new teachers and most importantly, we enter a new experience. The experience we endure and hold on to is what helps us remember the lessons we learned. We learn from our experiences and every day, we live in the moment by creating a new one. We learn to communicate more and open our mind to all the possibilities. We learn to allow ourselves to see more than we thought that we could.

Every step we take doesn't have to be taken alone, we take these steps together and eventually come to a point where we can grow and learn to take those steps alone. We begin to develop the strength to carry on in life, we begin to discover our own skills that contribute and help others and ourselves. Life is the bridge that never ends. It keeps on going till the end of our time.

Time is what we are always chasing, wondering when it will freeze and when it will ever wait for us. We remember who we were and what kind of childhood we had. Who were the people we were once friends with and who were the friends that we looked up to for support and help? What were the memories of our childhood that helped us learn? Life is a struggle that isn't always a challenge, we can choose to enter it alone or we can overpower it and use it as a guideline to direct us on that bridge that we take. People don't seem to realize that life goes on and the moment, whether it's a good or bad one, will eventually pass. We begin to walk along our bridge and then run and eventually one day, when were ready we will fly.

The bridge is there as our guideline, a guideline to improve mistakes, to better ourselves and to achieve greatness. We are made and created to be different, to carry unique qualities, to have different personalities but we are destined so that one day whether we are lost or stranded, we learn to cross that bridge. We are given the opportunity to come along once we learn how to control and conquer our life. Our memories and experiences that we carry along with us stick with us because the hidden lessons behind them are the important parts of life that make it impossible to let go of. Whether we learn to use life as a contributing factor for great success or we try to tear it down, the bridge will always exist. If it is not seen, it will be noticed as a pathway of who we really are when we struggle to figure out who we are and if we fit in. One day, we will learn to enter a new door and take a new path leading us to endless possibilities taking us to unknown places that we ourselves have never dreamed of.

A PARTIAL RECOVERY

My name is Nicholas for those of you who don't know me. And guess what I've learned? Life sucks, it can be your most hateful and deadliest enemy or it can be your best friend. But don't get too attached before it takes over who you are. About a year ago, I suffered almost each day and night asking for a wish and hoping for an answer. I spent those dreadful nights locked up in my room excluding myself from the outside world. I wanted to remain hidden; I only did it because I was scared. I feared those who made me insecure and upset about being myself. I would do anything to just fit in. Wear the clothes, talk the slang and act as if I was someone else, someone who I pretended to be. Act, that's the keyword that resonates with me over and over again because we all live behind a mask, we all have done something out of the extraordinary and still, we struggle to drop the act. Even till this day I still act, I try not to be myself but I'm insecure that society won't be as friendly to those who are different. One thing hit me the other day when someone told me to be myself, to learn to love life. At first I thought they were crazy, maybe even stupid, but now I look past that I have developed a deeper understanding only to what they truly meant. Life does go on, but remember you live it once. So with everything that you do in life, remember to treasure it and hold on to every moment as if it was like your last breath. Breathe life, feel it and live it. I know it probably sounds crazy but I found that when you love life, things come easier such as friends or happiness.

YOU ARE A BEAUTIFUL CREATION

When we feel like giving up, we choose to live our life in fear. When people say how horrible or depressing their life is, always look at life as an experience. You see part of what makes life a challenge is having obstacles in it. We are challenged to see how well we are able to cope with the obstacles life throws at us. Never look at something as a negative impact because every impact in our life is there for a reason. Whether it is a good or bad reason, we learn from our mistakes which helps us become the person we are today. Obstacles we face are there to show us how strong we are inside and out and knowing that we can be all that is possible. Life is such a beautiful thing that most of us take for granted. We see it as being a waste or just pointless. That's not true, we are all important and we serve a purpose. Whether it's being that role model to others or giving someone hope, we all shape the world to make it that wonderful place. Beauty is always everlasting and can always be searched for even within the darkest places.

When you feel alone, depressed, angry always remember that life gets better. The negative feelings that we let hold us back affect us in the most severe way possible. Why do we? People are only trying to make us feel insecure by lowering our self-esteem. Life is always brighter on the other side, we may meet people whom we love and make the best come out of us. But then there are those people who we can just be ourselves with, whether it's being that goofy person or having that shy personality, it's the person who we truly are. In life, people will only try to discourage you for two reasons - number one, because you have something that they are jealous of and number two, because you're everything that they want to be.

VOICELESS

You're that beautiful, intelligent, happy person who learns to love life and who doesn't care how people make you feel. You are beautiful inside and out no matter what people say, whether you're skinny, fat, short or tall. You are beautiful just like that flower that blossoms in the midst of the garden. Just like that smile that forms within your heart, you are the chosen creation of God. Don't ever let anyone tell you different. Learn to be yourself because by doing that you never have to live behind a mask. To the people who made you feel that you were nothing, feel remorseful for them and even try to help them. They too need love from someone in some shape or form.

When people try to bring us down, look at it as a way to become stronger and as an opportunity to show them that you are the person they wish they could be. No matter what happens in life, we learn from our mistakes. Every time we learn, it only makes us more capable to deal with people, society and what the world throws at us. So no matter what, always remember, you are not alone and are perfect in every way you can be.

STRUGGLING TO BE THE VOICE

Don't ever let anyone discourage you or make you believe different.

Don't let anyone take away a part of you that makes you so wonderful and unique. It's that part of you that they want to have. Always hold your head up high in knowing you are such an amazing person. When life makes you put up with mean and hurtful people, always remember there is a time for change, a time to mourn, and a time to feel wanted. So to those people who make you feel insecure by lowering your self-esteem, all you can say to them is thank you for making you a stronger person and for helping you see that you are exactly what you were meant to be. Don't ever doubt life because it takes you places you could never imagine. But we should all remember that life faces us with difficulties that will try to bring us down; the only thing we can do is keep moving forward.

FINDING OUR SENSE OF BELONGING

Every one of us has wanted to change their perspective on what they see to be normal in hopes to become more open-minded. We all have once obtained that thought that we need to fit in. Or we need to find a place of belonging but it is only when we look and wonder who we really are, we begin to develop a sense of belonging. To be accepted is one of our fears. We hate what people see about us on the outside rather than getting to know our personality. People are always curious about making choices, we always tend to perceive that every choice is a wrong one, but when it comes to fitting in it's not a choice of right or wrong, it's a chance for us to reach our full potential. To feel pride, to have a friend to walk to class, to have somebody make us laugh and most importantly, to find that one person whom we see inside and out for what they really are, a true friend. We search to find friends, just wanting to belong to something. But the question of a true friend always remains unanswered. Fitting in is just a part of life whether it involves how we look or how we speak or where we stand as a person. People always seem to find something about us that they believe is unacceptable and unwanted and we too tend to believe that. If only we could come back to reality and realize that the opinion of another is just a thought, nothing to fear or worry about. It is those portraying and ignorant thoughts that make us believe that we ourselves will always be unknown and not accepted. We make ourselves feel as if we do not belong to society when it was not even a thought that we should have. So whether you talk differently or have different likes or interests, we might always feel unaccepted. Feeling unaccepted and unwanted is what we all fear. We all want to have the looks and the popular friends but when we look to discover a special gift in each other we begin to develop a passion for that person and show our appreciation. Feeling as if you need to have the luxury to our ordinary lives to be accepted is nothing more but unnecessary. Some of us may change the way we look because we aren't happy, we may try to do whatever it takes to belong in that group of friends or with those people but if we really focus and see who we really are, we begin to realize that not being ourselves is what makes us unsure and curious. Still searching for our true self, still trying to find our sense of belonging in the world.

SURVIVOR

Doesn't it ever occur to you that people always act and pretend to be someone other than who they really are? They underestimate and misunderstand people who love life. The ones who make every moment last, every memory worth remembering. Does that make me different because I like to have fun or because I like to be me? Why am I any different from the norm because I talk to everyone, because of how I dress? Nowhere does God tell us to judge without knowing. He said, "Love everyone", in other words, "Love thy neighbor as you love thy self". I am an aspect of His creation and sometimes I need someone to remind me of that. I may cry or scream when no one's around but that's because I'm human. Who says I can't laugh or party or have fun without being misjudged?

Rumors are the exact opposite of the truth; they make someone feel different, unaccepted and make me feel like I live under a shadow. High school is still a battle I face, but I know with God by my side, no one and nothing can stop me from doing what I want. Do you know what I say to those people who think of me differently? "Have a great life" because I know that in every moment I live mine, I know that I can live my life in harmony with no troubles or worries unlike others who have to suffer living behind a mask. My best friend once told me that we all live under a mask. That we try to fit in, I was once that person, but now I am myself. Forever and ever in our life people will tell us how we should live and what we can't do than what can we do. I'm tired of feeling invisible, I want to be noticed. I'm tired of the rumors, and most importantly I'm hurt that people negatively speak about me. Just when my life was getting better, things got worse. I know for a fact that God gives me the courage to overcome my fears. Now it's time to deal with matters in my own hands. I need to fight for Nicholas because if I don't nobody will. I need to feel that power of God within me to tell others how I feel about the matter. To them, it might be fun to gossip but for me having to live with that rumor defining me, blocks me from coming out from my shadow. The struggle I face is just a chapter to my story but it will get better. I will continue to be happy and no one can stop me.

VOICELESS

My friends, family, and even my parents are drifting away as I continue to get older. As I get older, it seems as if life gets harder. Why does life have to go by so quickly? I could just end the pain with thoughts of suicide. I want to be known as the survivor, the one who made it and was able to overcome the challenge of bullying. I don't want to run away anymore, I rather would fight back. If that's what it takes to straighten out this matter, I will do it. It's the struggle I face and the battle I fight and it's something I have to do. I have to tell people and make them aware that I exist and I cannot be broken. I won't be. I know who I am and no one can tell me I'm something else. Some days I feel as if my future will get better, maybe I could be that inspiration to other kids. The survivor because bullying has become such a worldwide problem.

DO YOU SEE ME?

Do I ever fit in? Do people see me? I act as if nothing is troubling me, as if everything is okay but if you really know me what would you say? I walk throughout the hallways as I'm given the look. The one that makes me feel like an outcast. People stare and talk about me, they laugh and think it's funny. Most importantly, they never seem to realize the effects their behavior creates on me. My soul feels as if it has been torn apart, I can't sleep and try to find that place of happiness in my dreams.

Knowing that it hurts, I turn to that one person whom I rejected and forgot to remember when he brought happiness, joy, and glory in my life. If only you could see me beyond looks, beyond my outer image and look closer. Take that initiative to get to know me. If you think it was funny to tell your friends that I was different and say rumors that I knew in my heart could never be true, it wasn't. As you were there laughing and making me feel neglected by excluding me, I sat there in my room. I cried and couldn't help but feel that I was worthless. I had neglected my family, and as I cried God heard me as he told me that he was there and one day everything would be over. That very next day I finally understood what he meant.

VOICELESS

UNNOTICED

When do things ever feel right? Who can I really call a friend when all that really happens is melodramatic situations and problems that somehow I get caught up in. People look at me as something different. A friend, a smile and a heart-warming personality makes me feel welcomed by their presence. Still I have much more to me that cannot be understood nor comprehended in any matter seen. People want to be my friend, they want to get to know me but on the inside, I am hurting. I see them in the hallway and avoid saying hello. I avoid eye contact. I act as if they are invisible, kind of how I once felt. It's not that they have done anything wrong, it's just that in some ways I'm scared to let people know the real me. Waiting is all I can do now and eventually this moment will pass.

FAR FROM PERFECT

When I was in grade eleven, I learned that I was far from perfect. I learned this lesson when someone said to me "No one likes you". I tried to be a good

STRUGGLING TO BE THE VOICE

friend but it was bad choices that led me to be friends with people who were not uplifting me. Certain people are bound to turn on you and they have a way of impacting other people to feel the same way about you. There are two types of people - ones who affect you and ones who infect you. Recognize the difference between these people because it affects you both physically and spiritually. Spiritually, you feel drained and feel as if you cannot be yourself around people who infect you. No one is perfect but try to make the best of every situation. Try to see the brighter side of the rainbow and when we struggle and face those hard times, do not forget who you really are. You are worth every breath you breathe, every moment you live through. Do not let regret hold you from moving forward and reaching your full potential. Do not let an experience define you instead let it teach you. To be kinder and loving and to be a better you. Everyone has a dark side that eventually surfaces but regardless of who they are, learn from them and maybe there will be more of an understanding and compassion to the chapters in their story that has left them feeling angry or

VOICELESS

hurt. Just remember, they are not perfect, you are not perfect but they as much as yourself are worth every moment of life.

CHAPTER FIVE

Replacing the Old with the New

FROM VICTIM TO SURVIVOR

Every day I would go to school tormented, abused, sad, and confused in trying to find God through all the chaos in my life. Almost as if he disappeared or forgot about me, because it seemed like he didn't care. I was hurt and felt mentally damaged seeking no attention, satisfaction but instead cried every day in my room suffering from what people said about me. What was happening to me, and why wasn't I brave enough to say anything? I let people hurt me, I let them take control of that boy I once knew, the one everyone loves. The one that could make you laugh about silly things, the sweet boy, nice to everyone but yet I held a big secret. So I hid behind a wall of me trying to fit in, wanting to be a part of popularity, seeking for things that God did not intend for me to find. A lost and confused boy I once was as people saw me in the hallways and ignored me, laughing, making hurtful comments. Afraid of what people thought I hid in the only place that I really thought of as a sanctuary. The bathroom where I was alone, where no one could see me, where I was hidden from the real world; it was only when I stepped out that I was faced with reality. I felt invisible, unnoticed, and lonely. I felt that when I was with my friends, things would get better that they will always be there. We talked every day, we were all friends till that one day that rumor got out. The rumor that changed my life, the one that people even today choose to believe. That I was different, completely worthless and that I served no purpose in life. It was till that day that friends ditched me. The next day they ran away from me. Ignoring me and I felt those feelings of hurt more and more in my soul. I asked God every night to help me protect my soul and to not forget me, but to notice me. I began to ignore God thinking that he would never help, never make me happier and never make changes in my life for the betterment. Still I cried. Lonely, bullied, hurt I felt, I was just a boy who went through abuse but I know that somewhere there is hope.

STRUGGLING TO BE THE VOICE

I began going to school trying to boost my self-esteem. I walked alone in the hallways yet faced going to that class of torture but still I kept my faith. Remembering God and why I needed him. It was only then that I decided to go to my guidance counselor. She was the person who took action to make changes that would impact my life. I knew at that very moment I had made a friend, maybe even more when the other guidance counselors went beyond their reach to help me. She cheered me up with my favorite doughnut. We became friends, something I searched for but for all the wrong reasons. I could be myself around her, maybe laugh a little, act a little foolish and forget about all those troubles I faced.

Though at times I felt that there was hope, the bruises that wounded my flesh that had left markings still had more value to me, knowing who they came from, and how they got there for all the wrong reasons. Black and blue marks that made me cry, that made me feel real pain that made me scream on the inside. Still I stayed strong remembering God, I remembered that things will one day get better. I continued going to that class, having fun talking to that small group of friends. I felt accepted. It was only sad to see that people couldn't accept that I was happy, that I was finding God and that I was growing into a stronger person.

After a while, the situation finally settled down when my parents found out about what was happening at school, why I was acting differently and why I turned away from the people whom loved me. I still remember sitting there that day, coming home from school on my birthday. I went to school excited but came home disappointed. I had been beaten up, my wounds still hurt hours later. My wounds were still open. As I looked at my family, they were all so happy, I wished that I could be like that. That I could be happy about my life. Making that one wish that changed my life that day was unbelievable. As I blew out my birthday candles, I dreamed for change and for people to love me for myself and to see the real me. People stopped picking on me, they stopped teasing me, they stopped hurting me and all pain was uplifted. I felt happy to be at school but still I suffered from comments made by people in the hallways from rumors that still circled the school about me. Suffering from lies that could never be true. "If only they knew the real me" I thought.

That year I went through a few rough weeks of summer suffering from flashes of those memories of being hurt, having no one to talk to. Until one day I saw myself as someone different, wanting to make a difference in my life. I wanted a new start, to make new friends and this time I knew I should be myself.

Greendale Secondary was that school that changed my life; I was nervous about making friends, scared that people knowing me wouldn't like me. Soon after, I became comfortable with my school environment. People grew to love me. They could say hi to me in the hallway. I had friends to laugh with. I had a sense of belonging.

I will never forget that one person who changed my life, my best friend Candy. I asked God to send me a friend who could understand and love me and shortly after, she came into my life. She learned to love me for who I was. I loved to make her laugh, draw funny pictures, make faces, and share common interests. She was that one person whom I called a best friend. She was perfect in being herself, giving advice, understanding my pain and for recognizing that I was hurt. I will never forget those memories even as they still remain in the back of my mind as if they are happening over and over. But I am glad that I have them to look back and remember that is what taught me to become a stronger person and love myself. I learned to love God, to remember those people who love me and to be all that I am, all that I could be because being myself is a side of me that you would love to see. And that is what I've learned from one of the hardest moments in my life that no matter where we go in life, we should always remember God and the journey we walk with him.

PICKING UP THE PIECES

Finding out who we are is a journey we learn to take, and every step of the way we may choose to take it alone or together. Some of us are unsure as to what the future may hold. We think that living in one part of our lives is that part that will last forever. But in all honesty times change, people change, and most importantly you change as a result, you begin to find out who you are. It takes time to realize that it's okay to change because it is how we learn to grow. People whom we know become people whom we once knew. Friends, opinions and our decisions change over time. Discovering who we are is what helps us grow into who we want to be. For some of us, who we want to be or what career we choose to purse is still undecided. But curiosity leads us down numerous paths and we learn that it's okay to take different paths because along these paths, we begin to discover who we are. That person who told you that you were so special or that one day you would be capable of endless possibilities, truly meant it.

Picking up the pieces to our own lives is not as simple as it looks. It takes time, something we all wish we had more of. No matter what happens we learn to overcome challenges. Sure you may fall or be kicked down but remembering who you are and how much life has to offer is an essential part of true success. In life,

REPLACING THE OLD WITH THE NEW

mistakes need to happen so that we can learn from them. Over my years of high school, I guarantee you that I along with you have made mistakes, maybe some that are worse than others. But I learned from them. Learning how to prevent them and make better choices is what makes us stronger.

Every time you take a step back, someone will always push you a step further. Believing in yourself is not as easy as it looks, because challenge and change are two things in which we fear. We are afraid that with change, things such as people, time and everything around us tends to move, but whether we are ready or not, things move without us. Part of us thinks that when we are in that moment, whether it's that happy or exciting one, it lasts forever. Life and everything around us changes and sometimes takes the biggest steps without us. Friends, family and even ourselves change, but it's a journey that helps us discover who we are. It leads us down a path where we discover who we are.

Once we learn that when we get knocked down, it is the courage to stand back up that counts. When the pieces within us are broken, they can always be put back together. It's okay if you lose some friends because you will make so many more new ones. It's okay if you did bad on one test because you will excel on so many more. Having the strength to believe in yourself is what makes you stronger. It's not as easy as it looks - to pick up where you left off. Sometimes change is better and it needs to happen so that we can reach our true potential. Change brings new challenges and new pieces of us waiting to be discovered.

WRITING INSIDE YOUR HEAD

Creating a fantasy world in my head makes me create something special, and that is why I write. Writing allows me to pour my emotions into a poem, story, or song where I can escape reality and pursue a world beyond the physical realm. From my experiences, whether good or bad, writing allows me to create words that only I can truly understand. It allows me to understand the feelings and sensations behind the pen on a piece of paper; as I reflect on my writing.

REPLACING THE OLD WITH THE NEW

When my pen hits the paper and my emotions overcome my body and the words begin to flow, I am able to remember the sensations and perceptions of how I viewed my life at that point. Sometimes when I write it does not make sense, but at the same time it is fine because writing is a form of expression no matter what type of form or context.

I write because there are days where no one understands me and probably never will. In the end I am left alone to experience the hardships and the good times. Writing allows me to create memories of something new, like taking a picture. It is a good way for me to look back and reflect on my life. Many writers write about what they feel because they want to be the change that people want to see. Their books and poems are what sell because they let their emotions flow onto paper and people can relate to that. Sometimes when I feel alone, I sit in my room and write. I let all my thoughts run through my mind. I truly believe that being a writer means that you have your own world inside your head, a world that lets you be yourself and never lets you be alone.

STRUGGLING TO BE THE VOICE
OUR STRONGEST

I remember a time when everything was okay. I felt okay because it wasn't the names that people called me or the pain that I felt held me down, it was the way God made me feel happy. It made me forget about what really bothered me about myself. In a way I felt content because I always found a way to find humanity in everyone, no matter how deep my own pain was. I lost that. I do not know if I became more aware and less oblivious to the names that turned into threats and the pain that turned into bruises. It turns out I am nobody. "Go kill yourself," they said. Not knowing who I am or what purpose I serve to the world had given me a reason to believe what they said.

I look at it like this - that pain is inevitable and struggle is unforgettable. The struggle I am facing now is just a reminder that God loves me enough to use this as a growing process, both spiritually and emotionally. I felt purpose in the things that made me, well me. I lost that. They tell me I am a "Gaylord," "A psychologically messed-up child," a "Mistake". The problem was because I lost what was taken from me, I lost the chance to be happy because you blinded my happiness with names that made me feel like I was nothing. Words that made me silent. So I wake up each and every day reminded that Nicholas is "gay". If this label is what defines who I am, I know that the pain I feel is inevitable but the struggle is the stepping stone towards becoming the person I am meant to be. I feel alone but when I look in the mirror, there is a reflection that shines back at me. The reflection of God. I know that whoever tells me that I am a mistake is wrong because I am perfect in the eyes of God. God shows me that and his love will prevail through me. Remember, our weakest moments is when we can learn to become our strongest through perseverance and growth.

THAT DAY EVERYTHING CHANGED

After that day, we stopped talking and nothing felt the same anymore. It changed because we used to talk 24/7, walk in the hallways, hang out after school. But now everything's changed. It changed because when I see your face I cannot look at you, that day made everything change. It changed because our long night conversations turned into hatred and disgust. That day everything changed.

Ever had people, who you were friends with for a long time and then all of a sudden become your enemies? This has happened to me a few times and it always ends the same way, we go our separate ways. We go down two different paths because there reaches a point where you realize you are not in alignment with each other. This is how the universe speaks to you; it puts you in circumstances that show you for spiritual growth change is necessary. When we say something has changed, we are saying that it has been altered or made different somehow. This is exactly what experiences do for each and every one of us. They either affect or infect you but ultimately they change you somehow. That is why when you go through something that is life-changing you can feel the changes happening within because the universe is teaching you forgiveness and how to move forward. Most of us are afraid to step into change because we become so accustomed by safety and security. If change happens then there is no security and with that we step into the unknown. However, change is essential for growth because it is a sign of progression, it is an indication that you are learning. We all are here to teach each other how to be better versions of ourselves from the inside out. Change is essential for this to happen because it puts you in situations that force you to grow. It makes you expand understanding beyond what you already know. You might be going through tough circumstances but you will be a changed person for the better.

TIME STANDS STILL

Sometimes I feel it never moves. Like the world around me is always and forever still. Nothing seems to change because everything just seems so still. Time stands still when you become stuck in a chapter of your life. For example, maybe you went through a breakup or dropped out of school. Time seems still because your life is not progressing to where you want to be. So you feel stuck and days pass, then months, and soon years and that trauma or experience that made you still in time becomes your life. Instead of living by the story, you live in it each and every day. That is why most of us feel trapped when we experience life-changing or traumatic events because sometimes they leave us stuck in time. When this happens, we can go into depression or our anxiety increases. We no longer have a plan or purpose because our purpose is sidetracked by our pain we are trying to cope with. Imprisonment of pain is our way of coping because we tell ourselves that time heals all wounds. But by neglecting pain, open wounds never heal and over time our wounds get wider and wider till we feel trapped within ourselves. Time does not heal all wounds until you give your wounds the attention they need. If you let your past be your present it will inevitably become your future.

THE PATH THAT NEVER ENDS

This path I have created. This path that I have been fated to pass in which I have debated whether to pass. The dark cold bricks that I hold are cold to the touch and the red-coloured flowers unfold a different sight. On the light that passes through the tunnel day after day. In which I choose to standby but do not enter. The story of gloomy dark bricks in despite of the rosy red flowers foretell what will happen. And if by chance I take this path who knows whether I will fall or crack. And when I do fall or crack who will pick back up my pieces of what I truly lack. By chance I could be wrong. Maybe this image of light and darkness is perceived in a wrong manner. Or maybe I am stuck to believe that happiness and success can be found through one path. Though I shouldn't have gone over these hurdles and through these cracks, suffered these bruises just to say that I can. Whether I am ready only then will I truly enter. But for now, the path that I have created has been debated to pass.

GOOD ENOUGH

Anytime in my life someone or something convinced me that I could never be good enough. Ignorant to the fact that many of us feel like we must be ideal or well-rounded in all aspects of our life. People forced me to change. They may tell you that you are not good enough or can never be good enough but you always had the potential to be better than just enough and you still do. Society is like this, people tell you what makes you in fact you and what you can fail to accomplish rather than acknowledge the accomplishments. Nothing will change or be changed about you no matter how hard we try to change because change shapes who we may become not who we have already become. No matter how many negative contributing influences said you could never be the star of your own story or that you lack the potential to choose your path ignored the fact that you have so much more to offer. You were smart enough to face the unbearable obstacles which life threw at you. You went through ups and downs to never give up. Embrace the little things that make you good enough, because as a matter of fact, you and I both will never be good enough to others, but you will always be the best and truly number one to yourself once you start to believe it.

REPLACING THE OLD WITH THE NEW

LIMITS

I always thought that life was nothing more than ambitious and adventurous. That we are intellectual and sophisticated beings which we have been manifested in. We say that possibilities are limitless yet we limit ourselves to a career, lifestyle, and daily routine. We are told to be who we want to be from the moment we are born into the mystical wonders of the earth. Yet, at the same time, we are asked who we want to be. We limit the limitless possibilities of what could be. When I was eight, my mom asked me what I wanted to be, I said a firefighter so that I could break down barriers and any physical restrictions. When I turned ten, she asked me, "Nicky, who do you want to become?" I said, "I want to become me because by doing so I could be no one but myself." Then the years passed and I turned seventeen and she said, "Nick, do what you want to do, see what you want to see, because whatever you do I want you to be happy." And so I did that - studying what I loved and how I loved it because restriction has no name, it has no proper boundaries. It is simply a border we hold upon ourselves and we choose to believe that these borders, these limits are forever existent because if it was non-existent we would have nothing to fear. As if pain and struggle were as easy as joy and love. We choose to see what cannot be seen because limits have no name; they have no proper definition. In fact, they are the non-existent aspect in which we struggle to be seen.

TOXIC PEOPLE

One of the things that can be very harmful for our spiritual growth is toxic people. I have encountered toxic people. You know these people are toxic because you can feel it whenever you are in their presence. They are usually the type of people who do not respect boundaries or are intolerant by your words. They are the type of people who have nothing nice to say about anyone. Growing up with a family member who was like this made it very difficult to get along with them. Every time I would try to express myself, in a healthy way of course, they would always take what I said and blow it out of proportion. They are the kind of person

REPLACING THE OLD WITH THE NEW

who would ask all kinds of information about you and even go through other people to find out more about you. Then moments later, they would use the same information to discourage you. You see when someone is not in alignment with you but your intention with them is always from you heart. When your intention is to see the best in them but they cannot see the best in you that is a good indicator that that person is toxic. Unfortunately, no matter where you go encountering these people never gets any easier because they always find ways to see the things they don't like about you. This is how you know the difference, someone who is non-toxic will always try to see the best in you; they might complement you or hug you or make you feel like you matter.

When someone makes you feel like you cannot be 'you', that is a toxic person. Now not all the time does such behavior make them toxic; it could just be differences of personality. Even if they are someone close to you, one thing that I have learned to do is cut the attachment. It is not healthy to subject yourself to people who are not helping you grow spiritually and making you feel less than you are. Cutting the attachment does not mean that the love does not exist, it just means that you love them in a different way now. Where they have their life and you can have yours, and you can be all that you can be by doing so. I wish that someone would have taught me these years ago and maybe I might have avoided a lot of unnecessary conflicts.

I know that misunderstanding someone's intentions can lead to conflict. I know that toxic families, friends and people who you associate with can diminish your light. You start to see yourself differently around these people. You feel as though you need to change yourself to please them. But God never wants you to change; he wants you to grow because that is how you can give room for yourself to blossom. That is how you can become the best you. When someone says to you that you must keep someone close because that is your mother, brother, cousin, friend, co-worker, etc. Do not believe them because that label is just a label. Because love is infinite, go out there, explore the world and allow yourself to be surrounded by people who can have your best interest in mind. You cannot make someone love you, they have to have it in their heart to love you.

WHAT IS LOVE?

Ever heard someone say if a relationship starts that way, it will end that way. That is probably true. Although I believe in change and I believe that we are that change if we choose to be. There are people who catch themselves in a relationship with someone who continuously repeats old habits. That is someone who we need to question our relationship with. It is never healthy when we place our trust in people who will probably hurt us again; even after knowing that, we still go back to them. We go back because we long for that love that was only ever one-sided. Remember this, the people who you surround yourself with reflect the parts of you that you like and the parts of you that you dislike. So, if you are close to your mother or father, chances are that what you see in them is kindness and compassion and you too have that. But if you are surrounded with an abusive partner, chances are that you are with them because you lack love so you stay because you believe that they love you. Lacking love is one of the most hurtful things because you go through life searching for it, looking for it wherever you can get it and just when you think you receive it through sex, alcohol, or other forms you realize that all things pass. When the alcohol is no longer there and sex no longer numbs your pain, you no longer feel loved. That is why most people find ways to relieve their symptoms but they never actually get to the root of how they feel. So, they go through life feeling empty and incomplete only to realize at a much later point in life that they are still left feeling incomplete. I used to numb my pain. I used to sleep because when I slept I didn't have to think about the world and how people might see me. It was my escape from reality because I never felt that people could ever love me for me.

For years, I was in a toxic relationship. It started off as friends and when I was in high school it turned into toxicity. She was my friend, she was one of the most courageous people I had met. Believe it or not, at one point I really loved her. She was crazy and fun, she was smart and quirky at the same time. She had long red hair and was probably the only person till this day that brought so much happiness to my life. When I was six, I met her in my youth group at my local church.

NOBODY LOVES ME MORE THAN ME

Nobody loves me. That is what I used to tell myself when my father used to say "You have a comprehension problem" or the kids at school used to beat me up. Nobody loves me because there are days when I cry and I feel like God does not hear me. Nobody loves me when people say that they know me but they never took the time to notice me. I used to tell myself that no one could love me because all I had in my life was hurt. There was no trust because every time I let someone into my life they hurt me. So I shied away from friends and family because with no love, there is no trust.

No one loves me more than me. If you would have asked me five years ago if I loved myself, I would have probably said 'no'. I would have said 'no' because I was bullied and I was hurt. We are all searching for love but how do we get there? I have spent my whole life feeling little to no love. My mother and my best friend were the only two people who ever really understood me. That was love. It was love because they knew me.

Everyone should be who they want to be. That should never have been a battle that we have to fight for. Everyone should be able to live without judgment or fear of who they are. It's crazy to think that we are judged for things that are beyond our control. Race, religion, disability, weight issues, sexuality, etc. I don't know about you but my God loves all. I believe that this generation is here to change the status quo. To push boundaries that have never really been challenged. To make room for more light and love in this world. Social media gives us the opportunity to express ourselves freely and authentically. Fight the stigma, they say. It brings awareness and less judgment when we understand that not everyone wants to be like the masses or not everyone fits societal norms. That brings me happiness in knowing this because I see a world of differences that makes us more alike than we know, because our differences teach us acceptance for all things, for everyone.

Every time you look at yourself in the mirror, the person who you want to be and the person who you present to the world, should be the same. That is what is so beautiful about human expression, it is bringing the qualities that are from within us to the surface to be expressed. For example, someone who wears a lot of makeup or undergoes facial feminization surgery, it is their expression of how they choose to identify themselves as. There is nothing wrong about the way you choose to express yourselves, but people become afraid when they see something that pushes the boundaries of what society says is normal. This causes us to put ourselves in a closet and hide who we truly are. No one should feel like they do not matter. However, you should express yourself as the best version of you that you can offer to the world.

STRUGGLING TO BE THE VOICE

INSECURITY

I used to fantasize that one day people would notice me. Maybe I could change my hair or my clothes to draw attention. So I experimented with different looks, different skin lotions in hopes of trying to become a better me. It started in sixth grade when another one of my classmates told me that I was ugly because I had a turtle neck. The horizontal lines that ran across my neck made me feel ugly because that is how someone had defined it for me. Since then I cannot tell you the number of lotions and sweaters that I have tried to cover up my imperfections. The whole time I was trying to change myself, I began to understand myself better than I had ever in my life. There is no amount of skin lotion that can cover up any insecurity. Imperfections lie beneath the skin, they lie in the heart space of us. That is why words hurt because we feel it in our heart that the labels, stereotypes need to stop. The uproar from this generation is changing the social quo. We are saying that it is okay to feel different, to be weird, and not be understood.

REPLACING THE OLD WITH THE NEW

Many years ago, there was a stigma about being different in a culture that was so structured. If you wore your hair differently, you probably would have heard something like "A woman should not look like that" or "She looks gay". Today, people say that it really is okay to just be you. Now you see people express their sexual orientation with pride and people of color taking a stance alongside those who are privileged to stand against injustice. We are moving into an era where people are beginning to understand something that I call universal love or one love. Which means that our differences are not so different once we take the initiative to use our own voice to stand with those who are mistreated and underrepresented in our governmental system. It doesn't matter who you are and what role you play in the fight for equity. What matters is your voice to say something when you see people who are less supported by the system.

When you see people of color, specifically those of black or African American decent being mistreated by police or the justice system. Say something. You have the chance more now then ever before to have a voice. Freedom of speech is what they call it. The ability to speak freely without offending anyone or anything. So use your power, use your privilege and use your freedom of speech to speak for those around you. When you become comfortable with your life but notice that the world around you needs a lot of work that is when you cannot rest, because that is when your heart calls you to make a difference.

CHAPTER SIX

Be a Voice, Not an Echo

RESTRICTIONS: IMPRISONED IN OUR MIND

When I was just a few months old, I suffered a tragic accident that started with a metal toy car being thrown in my crib. My father had these family friends who came over to my parents' house with their son.

My mother told me this story like this, she had placed me in her lap and her friend suggested that I should be placed in the crib. So my mom placed me in the crib as her friend's son was playing in the same room as me with his toy cars. He picked up one of his red toy cars and threw it in my crib. That was the first time my mom and dad feared that my quality of life would be affected because of my hand that limited my mobility. After being rushed to the hospital and having numerous stiches, the precaution became that there could be a possibility that I would lose use of my right hand. My limited mobility never stopped me, because let me tell you today this hand works better than my left one. In fear of me losing my mobility in my right hand, my mom always had precaution when it came to participating in sports or writing in school. Somehow I defined all odds and I figured out how to write with both hands. I tried not to let myself be stuck in my circumstances. I think it was because I understood that all things are possible with God. That even if there was a slight chance my hand would get better, I would still be able to do anything.

It wasn't until a few years later when I was in grade three, some of the other kids in my school found out about my hand being operated on. Knowing this, one day when I was headed to the gymnasium, a few of the kids slammed my hand between the latch and the door and kicked the door repeatedly. I didn't think much about it until my mom found out from my teacher and our doctor said that I needed another surgery. What I learned from this chapter in my life is that our limitations are the ones that we tell ourselves. If you tell yourself that all things are possible, that is your power and with that you have no restrictions. If you tell yourself that your restrictions keep you from living, that is your imprisonment. God gives you and me what we can handle. Knowing this, whatever your physical limitations may be, know that there becomes no restriction once you tell yourself that you can do anything. Remind yourself that there is no obstacle greater than the ones you put before yourself.

PERFORMANCE MINDSET

Living in a basement for half of my life has taught me that to rise above any circumstance that has held you down is to preserve in wherever you feel called to be. For example, if you believe that working in makeup is your passion and that is where you feel most driven to be, do it. No one will stop you because your intuition is always reassuring you.

My parents used to have this picture of a big house up on a mountain with trees all around the property and numerous cars in the driveway. My father hung this picture in my bedroom, and for many years I stared at the picture trying to decipher how someone could have that much money. The words on the picture wrote "Justification for Higher Education". When you see a picture like that you think that it means "Oh if I work hard and get a proper education then I can have the car and the house". There is this performance mindset in society that you need to be successful, to be successful. That is what we have been steered to believe, and so how you were raised not only affects you but also influences you to believe things that are not true.

What that picture conveyed is that you have a choice in every decision you make. If you choose not to contribute to society by not working, you make that choice and that decision affects you every day. Of course, there are circumstances where people cannot work due to disability, health problems and many things beyond their control. If you choose to do your best in whatever you are thinking about pursuing, that is your choice and the outcome will show by the blessings that come.

STRUGGLING TO BE THE VOICE

ELEMENTARY SCHOOL

When I was in Elementary school, I struggled making friends and I found myself isolated from the other kids. When recess came, I would hide in the change room because I never wanted to be seen alone on the playground. I wouldn't eat because the other kids would make comments about the ethnic food that my mother packed for me.

I would starve myself because starving myself helped me forget about my pain and instead I would only think about how hungry I was all day. In grade five, I made friends with a boy who I used to play with in kindergarten. I used to go to his house and play video games and watch television, I needed that because it gave me a chance to get out of my house. I used to think that mental or physical abuse is a form of friendship. I thought this way because when I had no friends he became my friend when I needed one. What I didn't realize is that what I considered a friendship was one-sided for him. He would yell at me and call me dumb when I struggled with schoolwork. When it came to working on school projects, he would avoid me for days just so I wouldn't ask him to work with him. When he got tired of me, he would tell me and then leave me by myself for the rest of the day. He used to tell me that he was only friends with me because he felt sorry that I had no friends, and that it was because of me people labeled him gay. What I thought was a friendship at the time was not and till today I don't understand why I stayed in that toxic friendship for three years.

When I reflect on this period in my life, all I want to do is thank him, because of him I was able to find myself. He taught me that there are times when you will be alone on the playground but it teaches you compassion for others who feel similarly. Every time he ran away from me or avoided me, I learned that if someone is not growing with you they are not worth having in your life. He taught me that the label of being gay is another way of saying you're happy because you love and accept all things. God created all things, and all things created have never been a mistake.

STRUGGLING TO BE THE VOICE
SEVENTH GRADE

It was seventh grade, I sat beside her not because I wanted to but because the teacher had arranged our desks beside one another. I used to share my notes with her. I used to share my jokes with her because that is what I thought was the beginning of a friendship. Then one day when I left to go to the bathroom, she sniffed my notebook and said it smelled like curry. What she didn't know is that the curry I ate at home was really good. Secondly, the laugh that followed with her malicious smile as she told the other boy beside me, it never left my head. I was angry at her for years because it was the first time I myself had experienced racism. I never knew I was different until somebody told me I was. It was that girl in the seventh grade who said that eating curry made me different and I felt ashamed for that. This is a clear example of why we need to teach our future children about different cultures and different ethnicities because then they walk into the world sheltered and socially conditioned to believe that the world around them is not diverse. Children are not born racist, they do not know what curry is until they are taught that it is okay to speak openly about someone's culture and food inappropriately. That is a learnt behavior. Racism is learned at home. So when you see children or adults who openly speak racial slurs that is their voice. That is the way they choose to represent themselves in a world that is choosing to move away from racism. Martin Luther King and Rosa Parks along with many of the greats fought for equality and when we are beginning to progress towards that goal, it seems somehow we are slipping back into dark times. These might be dark times but now more than ever, the world needs you to make it known that their work, the work of your ancestors will not be overseen.

We are not fighting a war with the world, we are fighting a war within ourselves trying to prove superiority or power because that is what we crave. There are some of us who are caught in the egoistic way of life consumed by money, power and privilege. The moment their power is challenged, they are afraid and upset that they could lose their power. There are those who do not want to surrender to equality because they do not want to lose their power. Once they lose their power, once people oversee their privilege, they no longer are advantageous in the system. But that should not stop you or me from speaking our truth from bringing awareness to issues of racism and classism because that is how we start the conversation. Don't try to change anyone or their beliefs instead try to transcend their understanding so that they can be more understanding towards others. Let them bring themselves to realization with time and hopefully understanding. Remember that you are using your voice to create a better world around you, for you and for future generations. That is the purpose of each and every one of you; that is why you came here and somewhere in you there is a knowing. Listen to that intuition or gut feeling and trust it, and allow your intuition to be your whisper from above.

BULLIED

It was my thirteenth birthday and I was in grade nine when I had my first beat down. The other boys used to intimidate me in grade nine gym class. In gym class, they would throw soccer balls, footballs, and volleyballs at my head. They would laugh every time I tried to kick a soccer ball and missed the net, or every time I threw the football and missed the target. What they didn't know is that nobody ever showed me how to play those sports. What they never knew was that my father was always working and my mother was sick at the time and I didn't really have any relatives who ever showed me how to play any sports. What they didn't know was that my right hand had two scars from two surgeries and the doctor had said that if I ever banged my hand I would lose the mobility in my hand for good. What they didn't know is that this was not the first time someone had decided to laugh at me or hit me. I never spoke back and every time they said more words that hurt me I was too afraid to stand up for myself. I was scared that if anyone found out about my hand being fragile or my father being absent in my life, they would laugh at me even more. Every time I would try to speak, the other boys would laugh.

STRUGGLING TO BE THE VOICE

One of the other boys grabbed my neck and choked me; that was the first time I choked on my words and the first time I felt speechless. It affected my life for years and I lived through my pain. What some of you might describe as trauma, for me it was solely pain because it came from a place deeper than anyone knew. Those boys never really knew anything about me because I was a book that was already judged by its cover before the story. So I got this label that followed me for years in my home and in my neighborhood. That label was "Dickshaw" a play on words, Dinshaw being my real last name. The funny part was that in elementary school, another taunt was used to call me "Dickless, Dickshaw, or fag". Those words became my label, they became the definition of me because I allowed it to be me. I wish I didn't feel the way I did at that time in my life but the knife to my chest felt easier to deal with than open wounds. I was drowning in my pain and had nowhere to go because everywhere I turned, there was judgment and with judgment came fear. The fear that someone would call me "gay" or the fear that people would not like me or my masculinity would be questioned. Even though I had practiced from the age of six till grade nine how to perform masculinity, it wasn't good enough because I wasn't happy and at times I felt I was losing my identity.

The other boys in my grade nine gym class would take their gym shirts and roll them up as a tool to beat me with. When I would leave the change room, I would have to walk past them as they whipped me with rolled shirts. The pain that I felt was greater than any pain I felt in my whole life. I became a victim of abuse and an easy target. As the year progressed, it never got any better; the group of boys just seemed to increase and I became insecure and alone in thought and prayer. At thirteen, I saw the world differently because the environment that was supposed to keep me safe, the school that was supposed to protect me didn't.

My prayer became, "God why?" Then it all started one day, when I poured my heart onto pages of my notebook as tears rolled down my face. I started to write and my pain turned into words that healed every time I wrote. Words that made pain seem easier to cope with. Words that started and ended with God. I titled it

"Struggling to be the Voice" and my writings became my prayer. My writings became my whisper from above because they allowed me to understand that I served a purpose in life and that words could heal wounds.

BIRTHDAY BEATS

My birthday landed on a Friday that year. How could I forget it? It was the day that I had my birthday beat down. I remember getting thirteen beats and a few extra for good luck. Three boys held me down against the cold gymnasium floor as one boy beat me. He hit me in both arms, my stomach, and back. I remember because I laughed trying to cover the fact that the pain was excruciating. I was crying on the inside. It was easier to laugh to conceal my pain than to cry and be taunted or teased again. When I tried to speak, the other boys would laugh so I stayed silent and in my thoughts. My head allowed me to escape my reality and was my safe zone, so instead I prayed silently in my head. My prayer became "Hear me, help me". I remember because the incident gave me numerous nightmares for the remaining of the year. In the years that followed I didn't have the confidence in myself to move forward from my pain. I was trapped in pain and imprisoned in my past because I didn't know how to move forward from a chapter that made me fearful. I came home that same day after school with a baggy sweater and tears that ran down my face as I tried to cover them from my family. No one noticed, and I tried very hard to keep it that way. I was good at pretending that everything was okay and then I started to develop two different personas. The frightened kid at school and the sensitive kid at home. My mother found out because my sister had seen the bruises under my sleeve. I tugged my shirt off and wept. It wasn't the bruises that hurt more than the pain of "Why me". Every bruise was a story, a mark to remind me why I couldn't be myself, why I didn't have a voice. My mother once told me that your tears never fall because God is always there to lift them up. If that is true, where was God when I was brokenhearted? What I now understand is that God never left me. God allowed me to experience this and it gave me a start to my own story and the words to heal my pain.

SUICIDE

I became depressed because the bullying had become a constant routine of endless taunts day after day. I was always home on the weekends with my parents while most kids at my school were at parties, or with friends. I spent years living in my room looking outside my window wondering what was out there beyond the clouds. I knew that there was something missing from my life but I hadn't figured out what. I remember as if it was yesterday, and this experience taught me to trust.

I wanted to kill myself. I wanted to end a life that I thought was not worth living. "At least I have friends, at least people like me" said my family member; at least I'm not "mental" is what they told me. What they didn't know is that every Friday night when they would go out, I spent it with my mom going to thrift stores and reading books. I spent countless hours watching movies and browsing the internet trying to escape my reality that felt pointless in living. My family never knew how I attempted suicide. I thought about it many times, but one day I decided to try it. When I wanted to kill myself I thought I was certain but I would always find a way to stop myself from taking my life. Then one day, I went to school and came home with black and blue bruises. Faggot, they called me and not knowing where to turn I turned to death as my escape. It seemed easier at the time because then I wouldn't have to live through the pain. The scary part is that in high school when you are bullied you really feel like that is your whole life. You feel like it won't ever get better for you.

That night I waited for everyone to go to sleep until I decided to creep downstairs. As I snuck past my parent's room I grabbed the biggest knife I could find in my kitchen. I crawled under the dining room table and held the knife to my chest as tears slowly crawled down my face. I was screaming on the inside. "Why God" I whispered. My hands began to shake, my words began to slur. When I tried to talk out loud, no words surfaced.

STRUGGLING TO BE THE VOICE

My speech was impaired, my voice was not heard. No one around me knew how deep I was hurting until the years that followed. I started to push the knife into my chest until it left a slight indentation, but not enough to cut me. I banged my head against the legs of the wooden table. Then I heard the words "You matter". It was probably my conscious telling me that but it made me stop the self-harm I was about to inflict on myself. I knew then that night that I would not die but a part of me felt like I was dying on the inside and my open wounds would only be healed once I started to speak my truth.

FINDING YOURSELF

Separate yourself from all things that define yourself that is how you find yourself. The true essence of who you are is spirit, beyond any name or sexual identity you are a spiritual being. When you begin to disassociate yourself from labels of any form, you strip away your human identify, but underneath all those layers lies your spiritual self. That version of you is the real you so when you feel like you don't know who you are, it is because you have forgotten what lies underneath all those layers. Underneath your makeup and your skin. Underneath all the physical parts of you that is the essence of you or the substance of what you are. When you become rooted in identification and social constructs, you have a limited understanding of yourself because you believe that the 'you' who has come into the world is all that has existed. But when you disassociate yourself from identity, you understand that the real you has always been there; it has just been covered up to shield you from the truth. As spiritual beings, our main objective is to understand how everything is connected. In some way we are all connected; there is a reason why every heart is able to beat and why each one of us has a story. The reason being that our human experience can help us identify with our true form which is love. The further you distance yourself from the truth, the more you start to live in the illusion of life. Your true purpose is to figure out how we are all connected.

STRUGGLING TO BE THE VOICE
WHO WE ARE

From the moment you are brought into the world, there is this process of identity. Where your biology explains whether you're male or female and then the naming process and then the construct of family and labels of mom, dad, grandma, grandpa, etc. These labels give you a human identity but we never really discuss where we come from. Think about it, isn't it kind of strange that from the moment you are created, you grow inside your mother's belly and somehow you end up here. You don't remember anything or anyone as if you had never existed before. As a result, you grow up thinking that this reality is who you are. That the labels placed on you are your sole identity. Then when you pass away people who are living mourn for your death, but we don't really know where these souls go. Christianity says you go to heaven or hell and that God determines where you will go. Hinduism says that you go through a reincarnation process and take different forms to have different experiences. Ultimately, most religions have the concept that if you live your life being good to others you are rewarded some way by entering heaven or receiving good karma. But if you have been bad, you receive punishment or judgment. My philosophy is that Earth life is like this, your human life is a high school experience where you are enduring all these experiences to become a better you. When you die, it's like graduation from the Earthly plane because you took as much information as you could and then go back to your true form where you came from.

I believe that a loving God will never abandon you, no matter how many times you sin he will forgive. I believe that God is from within and that is why God speaks to the heart. No matter how much bad karma you accumulate, it will teach you to transcend that karma and teach you how to make better decisions. A loving God never leaves you, he leads you to where you need to be. Whatever your religion may be, if you are Muslim, Catholic, Buddhist, etc. somehow we are all connected. That is why we all share experiences that teach us, that is why we all share one God. Our prayers might be different, our cultures might be diverse, our skin might be various complexions but our hearts all connect us to one God.

BODY IMAGE

Every time I look at myself in the mirror, I can find at least one imperfection, from stretchmarks to discoloration and even moles. My body is nowhere to being model material but I do know that how we view ourselves is how people view us. I used to feel insecure about my weight because my weight constantly fluxgated. A lot of my weight gain came from my grade nine year when the bullying from elementary followed me into high school and worsened over time. When I looked at myself, I saw the words ugly on my forehead because it brought me back to that boy in elementary who said I had a turtle neck. I didn't love myself until I realized that the kind of life I wanted to build with people lies skin deep, one that focuses on spiritual connection. The stretch marks on my thighs are a reminder that I am perfect. Imperfections are the gateway to living authentically and happily. No amount of Botox or filler can create the happiness you feel when you see people as spiritual beings. You begin to see that you want long conversations about topics you care about. You want to go out and share the same hobbies or explore life together. When people first look at you, they see your appearance but your spiritual connection is the connection that surpasses appearance. Soul is the substance that people talk about when they talk about relationships. That is the connection you make that see past any imperfection. Those of you who feel like you have no voice in a society that is heavily influenced by false perceptions of beauty, accept yourself before others can begin to accept you. Love yourselves even if others tell you not too.

A FRESH START

Towards the end of my grade nine year, I fell into a deep depression. I didn't eat or sleep properly, I had continuous nightmares and most nights would sit on my bed and eat buckets of ice cream. It wasn't until one day when I was lying on my bed, my mother said to me "There's a bigger world out there and if your happiness is not at this school I am okay with moving you". I wanted to stay in a Catholic school because I had grown up in a Catholic school my whole life.

After a long meeting with the principal and with the school's police officer, I made the decision not to return the following year. "He will go to the public school beside this school where he can learn about different religions, different cultures and meet all types of people," my mother said. The following year I attending the school which was directly beside my current school. That was my fresh start because no one would know anything about me and I would have the chance to make a good impression. Greendale Secondary School became my home because it was a place where I saw people who dressed much differently, who spoke numerous languages. I learned the most through this experience because it showed me that somehow we are connected. I started to understand that my mother's wish for me was to see that your environment can affect the type of person you become. It changes the way you interact with the people around you because for the first time I felt safe. However, I still had a mask underneath because I was afraid if anyone knew too much about me they would judge me. Or that the kids from my old high school would find a way to ruin my experience at this new high school. So I didn't speak to too many people, I didn't let them know my story instead I decided to write my stories that way no one would know what I was thinking or how much I was hurting on the inside.

DOCUMENTING EXPERIENCES

As I started to document my experiences throughout high school and up till university, my writings became a way for me to escape from my pain. It allowed me to express myself secretly so that I wouldn't have to carry the weight of grief. I started to create poems and short stories that were real incidences that were a part of my experiences. I never knew how I was able to create some of the most inspirational pieces but I believe that somehow as the words hit the paper I was creating content that was deeply rooted in spirituality. Most of the time, my short stories didn't make sense and often I would scratch out ideas or thoughts that I couldn't bring together.

As the years went by, I got really good at writing short stories because writing them became a routine for me. When I was experiencing struggles that made me feel stuck in my life, my writings helped me find a way to move forward and let the past go. With over ninety pages of writings, somehow I was able to bring the content together to create "Struggling to Be the Voice". It was my first writing piece, the one that started this journey for me and the first time I found a place of solitude in my head. It led to a better me because I knew that one day these short stories could be shared with people to enlighten them in their own life.

I strongly believe that accidents do not happen without reason, and somewhere in me there is this knowing that this has always been my purpose Somehow I found the strength to love myself more than I did eight years ago, and every writing piece allowed me to understand the positive of every experience. I discovered that there was a light in me and it allowed me to turn an unfortunate event or experience into progressiveness. It allowed me to understand that within every experience there is a lesson. To understand the experience, you must find the lesson and learn from your experiences.

Years later, I understood that at the core of myself I am a spiritual being, just like you, who is here to grow spiritually. As I began to learn lessons through my experiences, I started to spread the joy that I found in the stories I wrote. I wrote for classmates and teachers and somehow each writing piece had the ability to connect with their heart. The writings allowed others to understand that there is a deeper connection between us, it is our ability to tell stories that connects us. For millions of years we have learned that our ancestors sat around campfires and shared stories. For example, Jesus who came here as a messenger of God whose stories have touched millions till this day. This has taught me that how we start to connect with one another is to find the thread that keeps us tied. To see ourselves in a higher light as a more compassionate and empathetic person, as we learn from pain within our own experiences and the experiences of others.

Stories have the ability to connect us and that is why the more we teach each other, the more we learn how to progress on a path towards enlightenment. History teaches us about past events so that traumatic incidences, where people have been victims of genocide or hate crime, etc. do not reoccur. If we are not learning from history then we are all stuck trying to move towards equality and fair representation of all communities. There is a greater cry now more than ever for more people to come forward with their stories to bring awareness to issues of discrimination. There are too many catastrophic events that have left so many people broken and hurt. Somehow we are more disconnected from ourselves now than we have ever been throughout history. Find that common thread and express yourself through your own creative process, whether it is art, music, dance or whatsoever. Tell your story and make it count. When the world turns dark that is the time when you shine brighter than before.

BUS FIGHTS

In grade eleven, I was failing majority of my classes. It wasn't because I was not applying myself in schoolwork, it was because I had given up on myself a long time ago and school did not attribute to my thirst for spiritual knowledge. It started in my grade eleven biology class when my teacher informed me, "You're failing in my class and if you want to pass, you need to buckle up". It wasn't the first time someone had told me that I was failing so I became immune to failure. Failure no longer mattered because at this point I was losing my identity and that mattered more than Biology class. I learned about toxic people through my experience of getting into occasional bus fights.

There were two of my bus mates who didn't seem to like me very much. We started as friends and shortly after became enemies. It all happened because a rumor spread about one of them and somehow they came to the conclusion that I was the one spreading the rumor. A friendship broke that shouldn't have but it taught me patience. Every day after school, I would turn on my Android phone and listen to music. This became my ritual because it allowed me to go inside my head and that was my escape. I would get onto my bus and that's when it would all start. I would sit directly behind the bus driver, because that is where the bus driver could protect me. Then moments later, I would feel a cold damp press against the back of my skull. The other kids would take tinfoil that they picked off the floor of the bus and throw it at me. On a good day, they would talk about me at the back of the bus with all the other kids till each one of them no longer spoke to me. When I tried to speak up, they would speak louder than me. In just a few seconds, I would hear numerous voices yelling at me, some of them were people I had no relation with but they had a greater influence on other kids in getting them to dislike me. My voice could not be heard over everyone overpowering me and their words seemed to echo from the back of the bus to the front. I would bite my tongue and chew on the side of my sweater. My prayer was "God you know my heart". Each night I would pray the same line over and over "God you know my heart" and moments later "God you know my heart". It reached a threshold point, that halfway through the semester I became tiresome of the bullying. I started to yell back and even if I wasn't going to be heard it didn't matter because I knew that I needed to defend myself instead of staying silent.

So one day, I entered the bus and sat at the back of the bus where I knew something was about to happen. I waited for them to make mischievous comments to me. "Eww" they said and "Get a life loser" they said to me. Moments later I snapped. I started to shout, "You are one of the most disgusting people I have ever met." I said, "You're a lying, manipulative twit." Suddenly, everyone turned and looked at me as I could hear the bus driver's voice echoing at the back of the bus, "Get out now!" I grabbed my backpack and jacket and walked the rest of the way home in the rain. I did a lot of crying that day as I was replaying what had just happened countless times in my head. I have to admit I felt a little better for a few days because it happened on a Friday and I had all weekend to reward myself for standing my ground. That same day I made sure to dance around my house because I had won, or so I thought I had won. As

STRUGGLING TO BE THE VOICE

Monday approached, the other kids got worse as they continued to tease me. And this time they would come near me and thump me in the forehead. I thought I had won. I thought I had yelled at them and they wouldn't tease me anymore.

What I understand now is that what seemed to be my battle with the kids on the bus was an internal battle. You see, I learned the most crucial lesson from this experience that the way we use our voice matters. The way we hurt other people matters. I was facing the same battle with the other kids as I was facing within myself. That battle was a fight to be heard. The way I used my voice was to hurt other people because I thought that would bring me happiness. "Be a man" they tell you but being a man means handling yourself diligently and respecting those around you. Using your voice to infect other people will only spread the disease, it will only make it worse because your voice is a fight for power. Anger vs. anger. If we want to be heard, it means using our words to say what you mean in a way that doesn't infect others in that process. Sure, you might feel better momentarily when you seek revenge or when you settle scores with someone. It never feels any better when you come home and lie in your bed knowing how many people you have hurt.

Whenever there is anger, there is danger and that is your indication that you must remove yourself from that environment. This is evident when people say "don't you have a heart" because what they are truly asking you is if you have the qualities of compassion, empathy, apathy, and love. They are trying to find the morality in you. Remember to be a voice that you want other people to hear is to speak with the strength to say what you mean in a way that does not offend others.

YOU NEVER BELIEVED IN ME

When I was in university, I had this professor who told me, "No, I don't think you have the capability." Those words made me clench my teeth and bite my lip every time I saw him. Let me take you a few months back to explain why these were his words that scarred me. It started on the first day of class at the beginning of the second semester. All I can remember is being afraid because he always had an alternative motive to why he said or did certain things. "Hello Nicholas," he said. My chest sank. I was nervous, new teacher, smaller class size, and the other students had much better marks. "Ah Nicholas, you will struggle in this course because you have a sixty something in the prerequisite." My hand started to twitch as I started to sink down into my chair. I stayed quiet for the remainder of the class. He handed me the course syllabus. I grabbed it and sprinted out of the room. That night my thoughts were, "Yes I do. A sixty something does not mean I cannot do this course." As the semester proceeded, nothing seemed too out-of-the-ordinary but there were strange scenarios that began to happen. It started with the class presentations. I wasn't really good with presentations because I always got nervous and ended up stuttering on my words. Consequently, we would have to do class presentations as a part of the course. I had everything on the paper in my hand but for some reason I couldn't bring my thoughts together. My anxiety ran high and my throat dried when he said, "No, No, No. Do you even know what you're doing?"

Suddenly, the air felt cold around me and goosebumps appeared on my skin. Then he started to appear in my emails as he wrote "You must present on this day just me and you". That was when his alternative motive became apparent. I started to meet with him to present and that was when he started to roll his eyes. When I made a mistake he would laugh. When I stuttered on my words he would place his left elbow on the desk in front of him and shake his head. When I tried to speak he would rub his forehead in boredom. What he didn't know is that when I faced the board under my breath my prayer was "God", as I whispered to myself. When I turned around and faced him directly was when he threw loose pages at me. "No, No, No," he said. I felt powerless but somehow I got the words to defend myself. "From the first day of class you never believed in me," I said. "You're right I didn't and I still don't," he said. "You never believed that I had the capability," I said. "You're right I didn't," he said as he threw the pages of loose paper at me. As the pages hit the ground, my heart sank and the dismantled pages looked a lot like me, messed up. My words became fluttered, "As a teacher it's your job to encourage and inspire students," I said. "No it's not," he said.

That same night I waited for my roommates to fall asleep as I crept downstairs. As my feet hit the cold tiles of my townhouse floor, all I could think of was how cold he had been that same day. That same night I walked by the creek closest to my residency and as I stared into the water I was deep in my thoughts. Then I sat up on the bleachers and cried. It was too late for anyone to be outside and no one was around. This was my perfect escape. The wind was heavy that night and that was good because my tears dried a little faster than usual. I started to talk out loud as I screamed, "God!" No answer. "God, where are you when I need you!" Still there was no answer. It seemed as if my prayers had been unanswered. As I looked out into the distance beyond the river, I saw no one. I took my nails and curled them as I jabbed them into my wrists. Tears rolled down my cheeks and onto the cold cement. I hated myself because it wasn't the first time someone had thrown papers at me and told me that I didn't have the capability. It had happened to me when I was younger when my father had thrown loose papers at me one day. And as the papers hit the ground, my voice stayed silent. All I heard from him was, "You have a comprehension problem." I couldn't read properly, I thought that's why. I thought that when this teacher threw the pages at me, I deserved it because my father had done it to me also. It was a reminder that I was never going to have the capability to do anything. "No, No, No" was the affirmation that I told myself I didn't have what it takes.

After that day I was never the same. I fell into depression for over a year due to the constant harassment I faced all throughout the semester. "Kyle has a ninety average," he said as he laughed under his breath. My prayer then became "God show me all that I am, all that I could be." In my prayers, I found solitude because I found a place in my mind that was beyond anything I had ever known. A place all knowing and unconditionally loving. I retreated to that place whenever life brought circumstances that left me vulnerable. I started to carry a rosary in my pocket for the remainder of that year because I felt like I had a piece of God with me. That rosary became my power that I walked into the world with. My plan from that point on was to never let anyone tell me what I am capable of. I knew beyond any grade I had the capability to do anything. When someone says, "You do not have the capability" what they really mean is that you do not have the power to do it. But my rosary was my power so I knew I could do anything. When you walk your journey with God, you have the power to do anything because your prayer is your power that you walk into the world with. The next day I turned to my laptop and started to type, I called it "Definitions of You".

DEFINITIONS OF YOU

We are so much more valuable than what people tell us. When we aspire to be all that God intended us to become, we are the image of true inspiration. I often feel that people do not understand us, but how can they if they have never known us. In knowing that we are that Olympic athlete, that Lawyer, or even the neighbor next door, we have all come to be an intention of love and understanding to one another.

People who are often misled to believe in eternal happiness without overcoming depths of pain are misled. People who intend to define our capability without coming to know our strengths are not knowing. They do not know us, and if they could they would not ever come to understand beauty without pain. As if we have no value. But I will tell you this, definitions are only a way to define, to categorize and dehumanize us. If every time someone chooses to define you, they will never truly come to know you. People will capitalize you. They will categorize and italicize the words that you say but who you truly are is outside any definition of you. I come back to a place of confusion when I realize that for every step forward, I must take a step back. To realize who you are, what makes you an outlier of the definitions that you are told to become. In doing so, you never have to wonder how to fit in or how to conform to the labels you are told to become.

STRUGGLING TO BE THE VOICE

JEALOUSY

My mother always taught me to elevate those around me and that is the key to happiness. She would say, "Jealousy takes you nowhere in life". Similarly, the law of giving and receiving states that when you give, you receive. If you believe that the energy you put into the world is the energy you receive, then you understand that in order for you to get happiness you must be happy for other people. Let me give you an example through a situation I encountered a few years ago. As I was working towards achieving my degree, the program of study had very few students. But one of them was always in an approach of comparison with me. He would constantly compare grades on tests, midterms, and homework. He would ask about my personal life and later respond with remarks such as, "Wow you're rich." Despite this, he didn't know that I had lived in a basement for most of my childhood and my parents had a hard time with finances. At the time, I didn't know it was jealousy because I was under the assumption that it was compliments with good intention. How you perform on tests does not limit your doorways in life. How much you have in your bank account shouldn't decipher how you choose friends. It wasn't obvious that he was jealous but eventually it became evident by repetitive behavior. He was jealous because when I did better on tests he would ignore me for the days that followed the same week. When we would go anywhere, he would say, "Okay well, you have to pay because you're rich."

You will know that someone is jealous when they are not happy for your blessings. Your personal and spiritual growth is not about abundance nor is it about receiving blessings. When you steer your life away from jealousy, your spirituality heightens because you understand that certain things are not destined for you and that is fine. Like how the Bible says, "God's will, will be done." Whatever you are given in life is what God believed you needed to help you be successful in your spiritual growth. Jealousy stuns your spiritual growth because you can never move towards the things that will make you happy since you are always in comparison to other people. Your competition should not be with others, it should be with yourself because you should always try to do better and strive for more. When you are happy for others, God brings happiness to you. I am a firm believer of this thought. I believe that happiness starts with you because if you do not rejoice in the success of your friends, family, coworkers, if you do not accept the way other people's lives are unfolding, you haven't accepted God's will. You fail to understand that for you to reach a state of happiness, you must not anchor other people's happiness downward because of jealousy. The universe has an interesting way of bringing clarity. It might not make sense why now in your life you don't have the things you want, but one day when it does you will understand why.

Even though I lived in a basement, I always tried to be happy for other people and their success. Remember, everyone has a story and even if you are not aware of what that story is to pass judgment on someone based on jealousy is not understanding that the rewards in life are their blessings from God. You might not know how they came to be a millionaire or happy in life. That is why our stories bring understanding because without them we would pass judgment. Knowing that there is a story behind everyone gives you the chance to understand how they surpassed obstacles to stand where they are today.

NOTICED

It was on a Friday. I remember because I walked to school that day and it was raining. As the cold wet rain fell onto my skin, shivers ran down the back of my spine. It felt like it was yesterday because it was the first time in my life I felt noticed. I remember wearing baggy gray sweat pants and a black sweater that was twice my size. About two weeks prior, there was an announcement on our P.A system, "Attention. Attention all students please submit all articles for the school newspaper by the end of this week." That was the first time I heard my name being called on our P.A system. That same day I went home and scrambled through my room to find my writing I had written the previous year. I found it on a piece of paper lying under my bed but some of the words had faded because it had been under by bed for too long. The words read "Strug to be the voi". It had sat under my bed for over a year now and this was my time to tell my story. I quickly went to my computer and started to type out my writing that I was going to submit that same week. As I started to type on the computer the words read "I was bullied. I was alone". My thoughts raced high as I realized that the moment I publish this writing, everyone would come to know what happened to me. Everyone would find out my secret and it would no longer be my secret anymore. The bullying would start again and I had worked so hard to have a fresh start.

I had this gut feeling that I needed to change the content. Instead of writing the article on my life "why don't I generalize the statements so that nobody would be able to figure out this was my story," I thought. So I did. I started to write the words that came to my mind "high school fills our minds with wonders and mysteries". The wonder was my new experience that I was having because it was polar opposite from my last experience. The mystery was that I could hide behind my words without anyone knowing this was my story.

HEAR HIS CRY, SENSE HIS STRUGGLES

High school fills our minds with wonders and mysteries. Friends are the ones that help make the landmark of what we call memories. We may choose to take the right path or the wrong one but the end result is unknown, leaving us with decisions that help us shape who we are as unique individuals. Friends are the ones who we share happiness, joy and laughter with. If we didn't stumble, we wouldn't come to know our destiny and that the people who we love and whom we call friends support us. They strive to see us find success that others may not find.

They may be the voice that is hidden and never heard. They could be that same person who we shared a giggle with or a smile but yet we never seem to give recognition to the people who show us gratitude. People tell us that we learn to grow at our own pace, that we need to make our own decisions, but why make them alone? People who are bullied or hurt may never give a smile or a hello and we wonder why. They keep their secrets hidden, things that you or I may have never expected.

Eventually, we find anger and frustration in that same person, the one that felt lonely, the one whom we bullied, the one who was once a friend. But life goes on, though the wound is too big to heal; when you are the person with the wound, who will be your rescuer to heal your wound? Although you're not accepted and are ashamed that you cannot show your face, it's the same people who criticized you and brought those tears that you must one day learn to let go of. If we cannot let it go, we must learn how to forgive those same people who hurt us, who made us feel insecure. Make your voice heard and speak for those who cannot speak for themselves. If you can change the thought or heart of one person, then why not spread the happiness?

We know that even in the darkest places happiness can be found, those people who make us feel that we are important are the ones who notice us. The ones who make us feel accepted are the people who we can then look at and know that they are friends. We make choices in life; whether we choose to turn left or right on that path of success, we will eventually blossom in to that beautiful flower that we always had the potential to become. As for the ones who we think are friends; they're just there for good times and for the laughs, nothing more or less. They are the ones who we know are tearing down our path of success. As individuals, we are more than capable of making our own choices and we are the people who are the decision-makers, the ones that can turn a frown upside down, crack a joke and make a laugh.

But in moments of despair and unhappiness, it's the people whom we trust and love who help us see the light that we couldn't see alone. To the people who dress or look different, we learn to accept them for their personality and human nature rather than appearance. There are people who we know need a hug or a laugh to brighten their day. When we show affection to others, we receive much more in life and the path that we choose will begin to slow down and stop for us to really think about who we are. But yes, high school's just

STRUGGLING TO BE THE VOICE

what you thought it was, a big rollercoaster where we find love, friendship, happiness, and joy. It is the one place where we can really sit back and think about all the memories that we carry with us for the rest of our life. Life really isn't the highest mountain; it's the hill that we learn to overcome and face together. We are the ones who shape and design who we are. No matter what people say, whether it's something good or bad, we learn to move on and make a change.

Although you might lose old friends or even people who we thought we knew, new friendships come along with a greater gift. One day we'll look back and remember the good times and the bad times. We'll look down our path and find out who helped us and whom were the people that we called friends. What was high school really about? It is a mystery itself and is filled with unexpected situations that we never thought to find ourselves in. High school is just the society we live in, the one where we try to find the place where we best fit in. And when we wonder how we went down our path of mysteries, we realize that life does carry the qualities of failure, friendship, success and love - all contributing to who we are leading us down the path that allows us to make our own choices, be the voice and take one step further.

TELL NO ONE

That same day, I sent a submission to my school newspaper. I went to bed moments later only to question myself, "What have I done"? I was up almost every hour that night waiting, thinking about how people would react if my article would appear in the school newspaper. The next morning I got an email, "Thank you. Your article will appear in the next school newspaper". I went to school the next day and as I was excited to hear about my article to be published, I was also scared. "How will people react?" I thought. It wasn't until two weeks later when I was walking to school that I got the reaction I had hoped for. My hospitality teacher walked in and placed the article on my desk. The first line read, "Struggling to be the Voice by Nicholas Dinshaw". "Good work Dinshaw you made the front page," he said. Suddenly, the world didn't seem as dark as I had thought. For the first time, I was being noticed. For the first time, my words mattered. It was the voice that I needed to get myself out of a dark place and look towards the future. That same day as I walked through the hallways, my heart thumped louder than it had before. "Thump. Thump. Thump". There were too many people in the hallway all holding a copy of the school newspaper. "Nicholas, that article you wrote inspired me so much. Where do the words come from?" she said. "Oh that was an old article I had written. It was about this other guy who I knew was bullied so I decided to give him a voice," I said. "Wow that's so nice of you. Really powerful stuff," she said. I went through the rest of the day the same way. "Hi Nick. That article was really amazing" to things like "Nicholas, your story related to what I was experiencing a year ago," my classmate said. From that moment, I knew that I had a power far greater than anything life threw at me. It was the power of God because somehow the words connected to the heart. Somehow, my capability was no longer limited. I knew this was God's way of saying "you're enough". It was from that day onward I committed myself to writing through stories that could touch people in a way that connected to the mainstream. So I started to generalize my experiences to appeal to more people. Some who could connect with the words through spirituality, religion, etc. Those who could connect with them through being an outsider in high school. Those who were experiencing life much differently than others around them. My writings became the secret part of me where I could talk about my experiences and no one could ever find out it was my story until now.

CRAZY REDHEAD

She was a Crazy Redhead with freckles on her nose and eyes that screamed mischievous. I had known her most of my life. I had loved her most of my life. She never knew that I loved her because I was too afraid that if she found out my secret about being bullied, she would no longer want to talk to me. I was six when we met in Mrs. Evans' class. As she sat beside me, all I could think was how bright her hair looked.

STRUGGLING TO BE THE VOICE

She always had a smile on her face with a hint of mischief written on it. She was so crazy that she would do cartwheels and flips all over. She would punch the other boys and try to light matches she found in Mrs. Evans' desk when no one was looking. She was a Crazy Redhead. But it was okay because she was my type of crazy.

I was six when I figured out hands are for loving not for hitting. Another boy had hit her because he liked her and she was more interested in drawing pictures with her pastels. As I saw a tear roll down the side of her left cheek, I knew hands were not for hitting. That was when I hugged her and her smile came back and the mischievous grin was still there. It was buried underneath her hurt she felt from the smack. I came home that same day and told my mother, "Mommy, hands are for loving. Not for hitting." After that day I never got spanked again. My mother never hit me again. All I got was hugs because my mother started to understand that we are given hands to touch broken hearts. My mother cried that same day. She threw herself in the corner of the basement and as I touched her heart I said, "Mama love me". That was my way of saying, "Hold me. Touch me" because I knew that hands had the power to heal. I went back to Mrs. Evans' class the next day and the Crazy Redhead was still running around singing with Mr. Edwards. Mr. Edwards was our music teacher; he would sing songs like Children of the light with us. That was my favorite song because I remember the words "in him there is no darkness". That was a reminder that with God, I would never be in a dark place. As we sat around the green carpet, Mr. Edwards started to play his guitar, "Trust in him, in him there is no darkness." As Mrs. Evans touched my heart, I knew then that there was something inside of me. I wasn't sure what it was but there Mrs. Evans was pointing to my heart and the chills that I felt confirmed that there was something she did to me. The Crazy Redhead hugged me and that crazy look on her face told me she was the one for me.

STRUGGLING TO BE THE VOICE

CRA-ZZZY REDHEAD

We grew up together in the same class and over the years she found a way deeper into my heart. As much as she touched my life I think I touched hers as we got older. She went from Crazy Redhead to lost because she never knew who she was. It was halfway through grade six that I realized I loved her. She started to wear her hair in a ponytail that year but as she got a little older, she started to show signs of sadness, almost lost-like. You could see it if you looked hard enough because she would no longer smile and her mischievous grin had disappeared. She no longer talked to me. Whatever happened to us flinging rubber bands at the ceiling or putting matches in the other kid's hair only to have their parent's, moments later, yell at them for playing with matches. I missed that because it was the crazy part of her that made me smile. As we started to get older, in around grade eight Crazy Redhead stopped attending Mrs. Evans' class. She disappeared. I had lost her forever. Every day since then I thought about her. I thought about where she was and what she was doing. For all I knew was that she had moved into an animal shelter because she would always make these cat sounds and dog sounds and hamster sounds. So we all assumed either she was crazy or that one day she would work at an animal shelter and would be able to communicate successfully with other animals.

It wasn't until two months later I received a message on Facebook. "Hey" it said. She never forgot about me. She hadn't really left me, she had just left Mrs. Evans' class to have a fresh start. She became my salvation at this time in my life more than she ever knew. I needed her because on bad days I would receive a message from her saying, "love ya". She never knew that I was being bullied. I never told her. She never knew anything about me because when I was with her nothing else seemed to matter. My story was the moments I shared with her earlier in my life. It didn't matter if people didn't like me or I was misunderstood or if I had no friends at school. What mattered is that crazy redhead girl was not crazy, she was compassionate because she was the only one who saw me for me. She was the person who helped me cope with mental breakdowns and suicide without even knowing it. I thank her wherever she is in the world right now because she helped bring out the humanity in me that I never knew I had. She showed me that we must look at someone from the inside first. She didn't care about my discolored skin or my weight or my insecurities because with her, it all seemed to go away. She was a messenger from God saying, "Anytime you fall I will be there to pick you back up". That is what she did for me and I thank her every day of my life for the memories we were able to share and for helping me find myself.

CRAZY REDHEAD TO LOST

As the years passed, the messages from Crazy Redhead started to drastically decrease. She would send shorter responses and give later replies. My intuition was telling me that something was going wrong in her life. Sure enough, I was right. That same year Crazy Redhead disappeared, I never heard from her for the remainder of the year. The following year when I had started at a new school, I was halfway through my grade ten year, when one day I got this message. It read, "Hey! Sorry I've been away for so long. Whatsup?" she said. I knew that I needed to respond because she was one of the few friends I had up until that point. She was my escape that no one knew about. I responded, "Where have you been". She wrote back, "A lot has happened. Call me later?" I responded, "Okay message me your number." That same day I called her and that is when I started to know that Crazy Redhead was no longer the crazy girl I loved. She started to tell me how she was moving schools and how her parents were going through a divorce. It broke her heart. It tore her into two because she felt alone but when she would talk to me she would escape her pain. When she was alone is when her reality seemed to haunt her. She had to come home to half of her life there and the other half with her other parent who was living elsewhere. Deep down I knew she wasn't crazy. I only called her that because it was the stuff she did that made me like her. I no longer saw that in her. I saw someone who was just like me, crying on the inside for help with nowhere to turn and nowhere to go. We were more alike than she even knew. Our stories were the same, both of us had been cheated out of life.

CHAPTER SEVEN

Wisdom in Your Words

RUNNING AWAY SEEMED EASIER

That same year was when she ran away. Numerous times she would run away from home and I would go months without hearing from her. I knew that when I didn't hear from her, she was not living at home during that time. For years I watched as she spiraled into a life with drug use and anger that she carried every day onwards. It was much easier to run away than it was to deal with her problems at home. Believe me, I know because I was doing it too. Being at a new school gave me the escape that I needed. That was me running away from my past that haunted me. Occasionally, I would get calls late at night of her crying and saying she had nowhere to go and how she didn't want to go back home. I felt her pain because I too constantly thought about running away so that I wouldn't have to run into anyone in town. I wouldn't have to see them in the local coffee shops or in the mall. I could have another fresh start once more.

She had changed that year, her words became flirtatious and her demeanor became malicious. I no longer saw that smile on her face and no matter how hard I tried to look for it, it wasn't there. She became Crazy Redhead. Even though she had lost herself, I still loved her. Even though she was going through life changes, I still wanted to help her because the thought of me helping her took me away from my own pain. So I did. I would meet with her whenever I could and hug her just like how she had hugged me when we were kids and I would tell her that it's going to be okay. When she would show up with bruises from fights, I realized that she had forgotten the lesson when she was younger that hands are for loving, not for hitting.

BROKEN FAMILIES LEAD TO BROKEN HEARTS

It was my grade twelve year when I had just gotten my license and shortly after my first car. She called me around May in the middle of the night. I couldn't really make out what she was saying because she was crying at the same time so her words sounded like she was trembling. She said, "I have nowhere to go. I have no food to eat. Please come get me." Without hesitation, I wrote down the address she gave me and started to grab as much food and water I could find. I didn't know what she would look like when I would find her or when was the last time I had seen her because it had been so long. I started to drive and when I got to where she was, I was not seeing Crazy Redhead. Instead I was just seeing crazy. Her lips were dry, her skin was dirty, her hair was oily and her clothes were ripped. I handed her the food I had bought and in a few minutes she had finished eating. Moments later, we decided to drive to a plaza and park where we rested for the remainder of the night.

She started to cry and told me how she had moved schools and that she hated life. I had never known why Crazy Redhead moved schools but it now made sense. That was when I realized that underneath all the pain and all the hurt was her heart. We laid inside my car waiting for the sun to come up with the seats all the way back and the windows down in the middle of May. I placed a blanket on her and my sweater under her head. As we looked up into the stars, we talked all night till the sun came up.

The next morning when I came back home, I sat in my room and thought about how Crazy Redhead was stuck in this chapter in her life. She taught me that broken families lead to broken hearts. When you don't feel loved at home, you go your whole life looking for that love you wanted. She wasn't running away because she was upset about the divorce. It was more than that because it was a cry to her family that said, "Why don't you love me?" She taught me that sometimes the people who we think are supposed to love us, don't. Sometimes the people who are supposed to protect us, don't. So we grow up never feeling okay and as adults, we live with that pain buried somewhere inside. I look back and think about the songs we sang with Mrs. Evans that said we are all children of the light. We are all just searching for a way to get there.

STRUGGLING TO BE THE VOICE
WISDOM FROM THE WISE

After my grade nine year, one day my mother came home with a flyer she had picked up from the mailbox. It read "Volunteers needed for Retirement home". As my mom walked through the front door, I ran down the stairs and noticed the flyer sticking out from the side of her left hand. That was my calling at that time in my life. I knew it because somewhere in me, I knew that is what I wanted to do, volunteer with the elderly. That same day I dropped by the front office to submit my application. This was where I needed to be, I thought. A few days later, I received a call back and after a few interviews my nametag read "Nicholas Dinshaw, Specialty Care Volunteer for Friendly Visiting" and I wore it with pride. Somehow the elders found their way into my heart and they became the friends I never had because when I needed someone to talk to they were there. They were the grandmothers and grandfathers I never had because they showered me with unconditional love that my own grandparents never gave me. They wanted to talk to me. They wanted to sit with me in the dining room, or hug me far too many times. They wanted to share their time with me on my Friday nights or Sunday evenings. The Retirement home became my sanctuary, it was my home away from home and the elders stole my heart. I didn't know that I would find my happiness amongst people who were almost four times my age but somehow I seemed to relate much easier with elders than I did with people my own age. They became the friends I never had but always wanted. Over eight years I spent bonding with them. The residents like Mingo who I would see right when I was about to scan my entry card or Ruth who was so small that her arms would wrap around the base of my hips when she hugged me. The hardest part is that as they approached the end of their life, it was hard for me to move forward because I had developed such a strong attachment towards them.

But the life lessons that they taught me throughout their own life helped me understand that a life without laughter is lifeless, a life without pain is pointless, a life without disappointment is effortless. They started to share their stories with me and gave me invaluable advice on how to live authentically. The best advice I ever received was from a lady named Helen who taught me that to live your best life is to "have faith, have fun but be smart". It doesn't really matter how much you accomplish throughout life, what matters is how much faith you have to understand that at the end of every obstacle is a rainbow. It doesn't matter how well you do in academia or how much fun you have, what matters is finding an equilibrium between them. Having a balance with all the wonderful things life offers. That is your best life. A life worth living is a life of faith that takes you to a place beyond your imagination.

We referred to Helen by her nickname, Queenie because when she was born she had nine older brothers and then her parents had her. Her mother said that she was the queen of all the boys. Secretly, she was an advocate for women's rights and because she had grown up with all brothers, she had to learn to grow up in an environment that was male-oriented. Queenie taught me so much in the last days that followed her life. Then one day on a cold February morning, I received a notice of Queenie's death. All I could think of was how she had found a way to heal me from the inside out. She gave me the chance to escape my pain, to turn it into healing through the wisdom she taught me. Her stories showed me that we are all subject to the human condition. It is inevitable that one day we will pass. You never get the chance to redo your life or to take back mistakes but you have the chance to learn each day as long as you are open to the lessons life is willing to teach you.

Most often, our greatest lessons are the ones that we regret learning. The ones that brought you to your lowest points in life. We didn't choose the circumstances we were given but we were given these circumstances to make better choices. After Queenie passed away, I put pen to paper and started to write "You know they say when you love something maybe its best if you let it go. What if it is someone?" Her eulogy became my prayer to her.

STRUGGLING TO BE THE VOICE

REMEMBERING QUEENIE

You know how they say when you love something, maybe it's best if you let it go. What if it's someone you love? That person you trust who you know will always be there. How do you let that go? That person I once called a friend, then best friend and eventually grandmother. Her name was Queenie. She is the person who I knew I could hear a story from and who could crack a laugh. Memorable times that we share with someone creates memories we cherish throughout our lifetime. Queenie was very special but I never thought I would have to let go of her so sudden. Then we look at life and realize that one day we will leave this earth onto whatever existence. So you know what I think? Make every moment last and live it to the fullest. Don't let people tell you what to do. Be your own inspiration. As I think about it, it was that distinct personality trait that I had respected most about her.

The Retirement home was the place that felt like home. That place had solitude because it reassured me that all I would feel is unconditional love. Queenie was my inspiration, she helped me find my voice. My visits were enjoyable with her and with every step I took, I remembered walking in with a smile and sometimes a laugh. Then one day Queenie passed. Though blood is thicker than water, I was there. I lit her face and every time she saw me coming, I knelt near her bed. Every time she gave me a hug and I would reciprocate the gesture by hugging her back. She always knew that I was special, and I think we both saw something special within each other. Some days when I feel hurt I am reminded that Queenie is no longer with me, I remember the stories she told me. I remember the friendship we shared and how she hugged me. I remember how she touched me when my life felt down. Being present for Queenie meant everything because she started to understand me better and she learned more about my life. She brought me closer to God with every hug she placed on me. God was always watching me and I think as Queenie passed peacefully, I finally figured out who my guardian angel is. I feel her presence everywhere I go. When I walk into school, my friends say that I am sad. I don't deny it but in a way I'm happy because Queenie is with her grandfather in heaven where she had dreamed of being since childhood.

Some nights I stay up thinking about why she left me. How could this have happened? Then I remember what she told me the night I saw the presence of God in her. She had said, "I will always exist in your heart." Unbreakable, untouchable and everlasting is the connection that we had. Some nights I pray to her because I know God is listening as he told me to hold her and to remember this moment. As I felt her hand shiver and shake her grip tightened as if she never wanted me to let go, and I didn't want to.

Queenie was the answer to why I volunteer at Specialty Care and she answered that for all of us. We remember people who we love and care for and share every moment with. I prayed to God that every moment me and Queenie shared shall be kept and protected. It started off as being a volunteer but when being in that position you wouldn't understand how you feel when you develop a bond with the residents. So as we leave here today don't be upset or disappointed. Do not shed a tear or cry. Instead hold that smile on your face as Queenie would have wanted. Think about her smile and her personality because it was admirable. It is in moments of despair we realize that people we care about the most touch us in ways that leave us speechless; voiceless. Let's take the step together in making this moment everlasting as Queenie will exist in all of our hearts making us feel her presence no matter where life takes us.

EVERYDAY STRUGGLES

In third year Univeristy, I fell into depression that continued for almost two years after until one day I had the courage to write about my experiences with my professor who had said, "You Will Never Be Able To Do It." I titled it "It's Never Enough".

That year I was tutoring at the Math centre. It changed my life for the better and below is the wisdom that it taught me. What started as Math lessons shortly turned into life lessons as my students would address all sorts of problems in their life. We would talk about relationships, jealousy and spirituality. I became their life instructor without realizing it because on most days we were talking about difficulties in their day-to-day lives. I didn't need a classroom or books to teach life because what I had endured earlier in life gave me wisdom beyond my years. Secretly after work hours, we would stay in the library and talk for hours. Somehow the students slowly became the teacher because they taught me much more about myself than I had even known. They taught me to love myself because they saw a light in me that I couldn't see in myself. That same year was the year when helping others get out of the dark place felt more rewarding than doing Math. When I came home, it never felt any better because I was sinking deeper into my depression. All I could think was "No, I don't think you have the capability". Those words seemed to be a lie that others had said to me and that I told myself.

It was a Thursday afternoon, when I had just turned up at work and one of my students said, "Hey

Nick. Can we talk?" I knew then that whatever the conversation would be I somehow would have the answer. "If I can't do Math at the first year level what makes you think I am good enough?" he said. His head turned towards the ground as the papers in his hand slowly slipped and fell onto the floor. I replied, "You may never be good enough or strong enough or smart enough. But you are enough." I went home that night and started to type the words I had spoken earlier into my computer and the words began to flow like water. I had a message of hope and if they were willing to listen I would be ready to speak. So I did and it sounded something like this.

IT'S NEVER ENOUGH

You may never be good enough or strong enough, or smart enough. But you are enough. One of the hardest things that I often realize is that the world needs more people who love. People who inspire and teach in ways beyond the classroom. What I am writing might sound like a eulogy but it really is just a way for me to utilize my experiences throughout the last few years. Being yourself is not always the easiest thing because even then the world is telling you that you are not enough. I am so happy that I have shared this experience with you because somewhere along the way the student became the teacher. You taught me to encourage, inspire, and to find new ways to enlighten your path along the way. Your path might not always seem clear but promise me that you will enlighten someone else's path, as I have done for you. Even though there are times the world tells you that the things you could dream and imagine are somewhat impossible to reach. Remember this that I say you are enough.

There will be days where you will stay hushed but remember to "be a voice not an echo". Someone told you that you were capable of anything you dreamed of and even when that dream seemed impossible, it was inevitably a part of your destiny. I often find myself lost in the lies when people tell us that our existence is invaluable because our strength is unseen. No matter how weak you might feel, somehow find strength in the things you know and with the people who have come to know you.

One of the greatest lessons that we can all learn is that we have a lesson to learn but whether we are open to paying attention to some of the greatest teachings life offers is entirely up to us. Your destiny might change and your path might lead you down indecisive and unimaginable roads, but no matter where you end up, never feel any less than just enough. Some of the greatest lessons I have learned are that for being the strongest at times your strength will feel weak so find that inner strength to persevere and God will take you places beyond any limits. For those who are always lending a helping hand, never forget that at times the helping hand needs help itself. Never feel like you are not enough because all you ever need is one person to tell you that you are capable of endless possibilities.

My Mom is the greatest inspiration in my own life. She has taught me some of the life's greatest lessons beyond the classroom. She taught me to find strength even when I feel weak, to always lend a helping hand, and to be compassionate to others. Thank you for reminding me that I am enough just as I have reminded you that there can never be enough love to share with the people who we create infinite accumulations of love with.

DON'T TALK

Her name was Tary. She was my manager at the time I worked as a tutor. My coworkers called me silly because I loved to find a way to make the students laugh at their mistakes in a way that made them want to try again. What she never knew was that every day after school, I came to work to be happy because work was my escape. The cold temperatures were usually the hardest to walk outside because not only did I have to worry about my bruises but also the temperature of the weather outside. Some days I would stop by the Tim Hortons just before work as I cried in the bathroom.

If I was more than one minute late, she wouldn't pay me for the full hour. If I talked to my other coworkers about what their school life was like, she would pull me aside after work to tell me "don't talk!" So I listened and every day after school when I went to work, I just sat still for four hours not speaking not talking about what had happened at school. Not talking made me scribble my red pen, I used for marking, onto tissues I found in a box on the desk. The scribbles were how I felt on the inside. That I was already dead. If I had bruises that day I just covered them with the yellow dress shirt and dark black pants I wore for work. She never knew how badly I needed to have that conversation with someone. It was easier for her not to understand than it was for her to try to understand. It was much simpler listening to her when she said not to talk than it was to go against what she said. So I listened and I learned that long walks to work helped me cope a little better and a stop in the bathroom at Tim Hortons was the perfect escape. What she never knew was that I would go home only to cry in the bathroom at home so that my family wouldn't see me hurt. Only to moments later write the words 'faggot' on my forehead and 'ugly' on my left wrist with my mother's lipstick as a reminder of how I felt on the inside. As I looked at myself in the mirror, my pupils started to dilate. No words came to surface because I had none. I just heard her in the back of my head saying "don't talk". At the time work seemed like the best escape but it was really only a cover that allowed me to escape reality, to be someone else for a few hours. "Hi, how are you?" I would say to the parents and students who walked in. That was my way of saying please talk to me, let me know that I matter. I never knew what happened to Tary after I left work a few years later but she never knew how much I needed that conversation. If I would have spoken, my pain wouldn't have felt so imprinted on me till this day.

THEY CALLED ME THE PARTY KID

They called me the party kid but they never knew why I partied. I partied because there were days that alcohol found a way to suppress my pain. Alcohol let me be someone else, it made me happy. So I got the label of a lightweight and the label of a happy drunk. The thing was that happiness was not from me, it was from a bottle that had the words "Alcohol content is...". That bottle became my drinkable water and at the time it seemed easier for me to drink alcohol and feel refreshed. It made me feel better than water could ever make me feel. Water didn't have the strong effects alcohol had because water only hydrated, alcohol made me feel like a new me. Somehow it was able to help me cope with pain. I needed an easy escape, one that made me fearless, one that made me feel I could be anyone but me. Alcohol made me friends, it gave me a new family of people out there who seemed to care about me.

So I and the three guys became really good friends over our drunk conversations and late night parties that we attended at least three times a week. As the semester progressed, we started to hit Rainsview Street where all the parties happened. Every night we started to increase our alcohol levels so that we no longer felt a buzz but instead felt drunk. The great part was that I never had to pay for alcohol because they helped to feed my addiction at the time without realizing it. My father always wanted me to make friends, my relatives always said "be a man". So I did and if being a man meant drinking then I had to play the part correctly so that no one would think otherwise of me.

It wasn't until one night when everything changed. They had purchased the bottle earlier that day but something told me that night not to drink so I listened. It was my inner voice saying not to do it. So I played along when we went outside for a drink; it was too dark for anyone to see much of anything. That was the perfect chance for me to pretend to drink. "Here," he said as he handed me the drink. "We already drank earlier. This is for you so drink up." So I pretended too. I ran away, dumped that bottle on the floor and started to wobble around because I knew that they would believe me. I was so good at performing since a young age that I would give them the performance they expected to see. That was the first night I went to a party sober. I didn't trust them. Not after what had happened the week prior when they had gone out with me and told me to hump a tree as they all held their phones to record me. I remembered because the next morning my housemates looked at me with smirks as I could hear faintly "he humped a tree". "Here's the video," the other guy said. I never knew if that video was circulated but I knew they had recorded the incident only to laugh at me. They knew that with alcohol, the words that would come out of my mouth would be happy because I was a happy drunk. Except the words were not really mine when I was intoxicated. My voice no longer sounded like mine because it was someone who had just found another escape. That wasn't the first time I realized what I thought was a friendship was only one-sided. I kept on going back in the same circle of friends because it seemed as if they were my family. "Brother" I used to call them because I hadn't had an older brother or much male figures in my life. Then the night of the party I overheard one of the guys saying that the Halloween costume they had all purchased earlier was not what he or the other guys were going to wear. "We all purchased it with Nick but we're going to return our costumes so he ends up wearing his alone," he said. They had a plan for me.

STRUGGLING TO BE THE VOICE

Moments later, a group of kids at the party circled me. I was trapped, there was no escape for me. "Gaylord," he said. "He's too drunk to hear anything," another girl said. "Get that brown guy out of my house," someone shouted from behind. They started to turn around and walk away. I ran out of the house and that night I walked alone. I took my shoes off halfway because my feet had started to hurt too much. I felt that I could no longer walk. I was sober and I had just heard everything. I took my time walking home that night as I held my shoes and looked up in the sky, I saw the stars only to be reminded that somewhere out there beyond the clouds behind the dark blue sky something or someone is watching. The moon started to seem brighter and the stars were a reminder that there was hope for me. Hope for me to change my life for the better and to move away from friends who were never true to me. That night I tucked myself in bed and slept with my window wide open so that I would sleep among the stars.

TURN IT DOWN

"Turn down your music," she said. It happened the following day. I decided to wake up early that morning and skip breakfast because I didn't want to see any videos of me or have a recap of last night. "They probably think I was too drunk to remember," I said. But I had remembered everything. The next morning I packed my books and headed to the library. I couldn't stay in my room before my roommate would ask me, "Hey, what time did you get home last night?"

I found this secret place in the library that seemed magical. I accidently discovered it that same day when the elevator had accidently taken me to the basement floor of the library. There were all outdated books, some of which were still intact but the dust had created a thick layer on top of the books. There were old printing machines and individual desks along the sides of the library. The basement was empty that morning so I assumed that not many people knew about the basement floor. I found myself in the corner of the library and the desk that I had occupied made me face my back towards the wall. This was what I needed so that I would be able to see if anyone came into the library. I turned on my phone and opened my music playlist. There was my prayer; "Open the eyes of my heart lord" was the first line that I heard. I started to sob. "Open the eyes of my heart," I said out loud. "Hear me God. Hear me hurt. Why God? I thought the bullying stopped in high school and now look!"

A few moments later, I felt a tap on my shoulder. "Umm, can you turn your music down please? I'm trying to study over here". She came out of nowhere; I watched as she walked away and sat a few seats in front of me. She ignored the tear on my cheek. She found a way to disregard my cry for help. Instead, the sound of my music was more important than my cry for help. I looked up at the markings on the desk and that is where I related my life to the words that I saw engraved in the wood. The words said "find your voice". That was me. That was me in the world trying to speak, trying to stand up for myself but not knowing how to. That had been me every time I kept secrets and I never let people too close to me so that they wouldn't know anything about me. That was me when I walked home the night of the party amongst the stars. That was me trying to find a place in the world so that I could feel as if I belonged. I was trying to speak my truth but didn't know how to. I picked my backpack and mug up from my desk and ran home. Things were going to change for the better and I wasn't going to let anything stop me. This experience helped me learn that sometimes we make mistakes. Other times we fall, it's the strength to get back up knowing that new doors and endless possibilities will always exist.

YOU WILL NEVER BE ABLE TO DO IT

Too many times people have said to me, "You will never be able to do it" and every time I somehow do it. We live in a culture that tells us all the things we cannot do but never really what we can do. This puts fear in us because it makes us fearful even before we can attempt to do anything. When I was in grade ten, I failed in mathematics. Although I was fairly good in elementary school, but as I got older I struggled with math. And when I was in grade eleven, I failed again.

STRUGGLING TO BE THE VOICE

No matter how hard I tried, I kept failing because I never believed that I could do anything. I knew I loved math but I could never understand all the symbols and formulas, so for me it was tiresome. When I reached grade twelve, I decided to commit myself to my studies and in the first semester, I decided to take math again. I took math at the university level in high school with a teacher whose words haunted me for years. It began in the first month of the school year when my math teacher gave a quiz that I failed by thirty percent. On the page it said, "Please see me." So I waited after class till everyone left and approached him outside the classroom. He began to shake his head and said, "Buddy, what do you want to do with your life?" So I responded, "I want to study Math." He looked at me and said, "Forget it. You will never be able to do it." I went home that day and cried. My mom came into my room and asked me what had happened. So I told her what my teacher had told me. My mother said to me, "You love math and if it's meant for you, God will show you the way." At seventeen, I couldn't comprehend what she meant by that but years later it made sense. When I applied to university, I applied for a math program because I decided to follow my passion. I went to night school and pulled my high school math marks up and received acceptance into all universities. I started university in a Math program and I said to myself, "I do not know how I am going to do this but God, you show me the way and I will follow." Many people started to doubt me and it didn't take much to make me feel less about myself. My roommate made comments like "You're a math major and you don't know math." When I asked for help, another person in the program said, "Don't expect me to be your saving grace." When I tried at midterms and failed, friends would say, "You should probably consider a different program." My relatives said, "If you can't do high school math, what makes you think you can do university Math."

I didn't know if it was possible for me to succeed but I knew that the path would unfold before me if that is where I needed to be. I started to spend days and nights at the local coffee shop, Tim Hortons. People would look at me as if I was crazy because I spent my whole day there. I would get up and go to Tim Hortons in the early morning and leave at two or three the next morning. I persevered and trusted even though the odds were against me. My prayer was, "God hold my hand and show me if this is where you need me." Through the years, I became a teacher not just in math but for life and I connected with many students and professors along the way. Slowly but surely, I started to work my way towards achieving my degree and ironically I did it. Four years later as the youngest in my graduating class with an Honours Math degree. The reason this story is relevant because when you are willing to try God shows you the way. When you don't try is when you give up on yourself because you have to meet God halfway. Up until today people ask me how I was able to get my degree and all I say is it wasn't me it was God, and because I have that understanding that I was supported along my path, anyone's opinion or judgment of me became irrelevant. This story stands true that "only God can judge me" because people will constantly tell where you need to be and what they would like from you. But it is never their way, it is only God's way. That is why those who seek God, find answers because they see it appear in their daily life. Next time, someone says that you will never be able to do it, remember to ask them to watch because they will see you do it. The universe is always working in your favor, it knows where you must be to be of service to the world. Your degree, job, business, etc. is given to you to do good in the world. It is given to you because God trusts that you will use it to make a difference and be happy doing so. But remember, the same way it is given to you, it can be taken away when you don't use it responsibly.

CHAPTER EIGHT

Whisper From Above

MAKING ME NEW

Shortly after I had distanced myself from my party lifestyle, I detached myself from the environment that was becoming an additive to my pain. I started to branch outside making friends in my classes and with people whom I met in the library. The basement floor of the library became my favorite place and I always sat in the same corner because that is where a stranger taught me the most valuable lesson to "find [my] voice".

One day around Christmas time, I was walking through the campus when I saw a flyer that said "Christian Group Meeting. This Thursday at 5 o'clock". A lightbulb went off in my head and right away I knew what I needed to do to reclaim my life. I went online and found the nearest church and came across a church called Roots. "All Are Welcome" the flyer said. Little did I know that the flyer would take me down a road of blessings and a place greater than anywhere I had been. The following Sunday, I decided to attend the church. I wore the best clothes I could find, a black sweater with fancy metal buttons along the side and dark blue jeans with sneakers. That same day I walked around the block and when I approached the front entrance of the church, my chest sank. All I could think of was that God was going to punish me for the drinking and partying that I had done earlier that year. But I remembered what my mother used to tell me, "forgive" she used to say. So I did. I decided to sit in the far back so that no one would notice me. As everyone closed their eyes during prayer, I whispered under my breath, "Forgive me Father. For I have sinned." I felt goosebumps run through my body. I knew that whatever was beyond the clouds could hear my prayer. It listened when I spoke. My prayer gave me power, it gave me the strength I needed to move forward in my life.

STRUGGLING TO BE THE VOICE

CHILDREN OF THE FOREST

I called them the Children of the Forest because they found a secret trail through the forest that no one really knew about. It made a ten minute walk to church, less than five minutes; it was a shortcut. Every time I would walk by the forest, I would see a group of boys and girls laughing and screaming words like "Woo hoo" that echoed through the forest. One day I saw them coming out of the forest as I was walking back to the campus from Roots. I knew I wanted to be friends with them because inside I figured that they were less likely to know anything about me because I had never see them before. "Hey. Did you just come from Roots?" they asked me. "Uhh yeah," I responded. "Next time come with us, we'll show you how to get there faster. We know a shortcut through the forest," they said. So we exchanged numbers and I looked forward to next Sunday since I could attend church with them.

The following Sunday I met with them in front of their residency at around eight o'clock; everyone was ready to go. We started to walk towards the forest and into the secret trail that I had seen them go through earlier the week. The leaves were bright green and were slightly damp from the condensation during the night. Nothing seemed too out-of-the-ordinary as we all followed each other in a vertical line following each other's steps to make sure we didn't trip in the forest. It wasn't until we had returned back to campus after the church service that I realized how beautiful the forest really was.

After an hour of service, we left the church together. The sun had just started to appear behind the clouds and shine through the trees. As we walked through the forest, the light shined brighter through the leaves as the clouds moved away from the sun. The trail had been more beautiful after the church service than it was prior to. Everything seemed much brighter and with the Children of the Forest, I knew that God was showing me how to find my light by bringing these people into my life. I thank them because without them I would have never seen a brighter road ahead of me.

STRUGGLING TO BE THE VOICE
SHINE YOUR LIGHT

In my second year of University was when I started to buy candles and light them. My window faced the forest that year so late at night I would sit by my window still with a cup of hot chocolate looking out at the moonlight as families of deer ran by. Most of the time I found a baby deer circling in front of my window. I watched as the clouds moved in front of the moon and how the deer stayed still in the moonlight. When the deer would come close to my window and stare at me, I would stare right back, and as I looked into its eyes I didn't see fear. I saw light. As the deer stared back at me, I believe it saw the same because it wasn't afraid of me. It knew that somehow the universe had connected all things to one another.

Almost every night, the deer would circle around my front window until the fall season passed and winter was fast approaching. That was when I no longer saw them. As winter approached, I searched deeper within myself to find that light the deer had seen in me. So one day when I was in town buying groceries, I came across a candle. It was white with a heart on the front and a dove whose wings surrounded the heart. Up until today, I don't know why I purchased that candle. I brought that candle home that same day and started to light it. Most days I would sit in the dark all day and have my candle lit in my room. Just like the stars that lived amongst the clouds and the moon, it seemed to shine no matter how dark the sky was. My candle was that star for me because amongst the darkness in my room, it was still able to shine. Most days felt lonely because weekends I spent in the darkness of my room. Somehow that candle became my light and I didn't know how to shine my light but I began to understand that even if you're in a dark place that is when the universe calls you to shine your light brighter than it has ever been.

My candle confirmed for me that faith is symbolized as a dove. A messenger sent from above that spreads its wings to open the true value of ourselves in order to find its inner-self. We are much like that dove. We spread love to many hearts. It's like us searching for God to guide us into light. Faith is something that every heart and spirit longs for.

STRUGGLING TO BE THE VOICE

Remember that within every heart unlocks the key to human potential that opens endless possibilities. The Children of the forest taught me this as well. That with faith there is no failure because you will always be shown the shortcuts and the faster roots than those who have none.

IT WASN'T SADNESS IT WAS ANGER

It was grade ten when I decided that I would focus on the arts. I liked drama but I didn't know how to act in drama class or how to interact with other people. Drama became the place where I learned about something called "willing suspension of disbelief". This meant that when you immerse yourself into a role, the more you become that character. It was about becoming someone else and making other people believe that you were the character you played. It wasn't a surprise that I excelled at this in my drama class because in my life, I had always been performing as someone else. I had a way of making people believe that the person who I was, was really me. From the laughs to the way I walked with confidence made others believe that my expression of myself was really me. But I knew it wasn't. I knew that I had always been playing the roles of different characters with multiple people and yet somehow, I didn't have the confidence to perform willing suspension of disbelief in class. I didn't know how to act because I was always putting on an act that wasn't me, it became too confusing to play another role. It wasn't until one day when my drama teacher said to me, "Hey, hey Dinshaw the audition for the school play is this Friday if you want to sign up." She handed me a flyer but for me that was pointless because I wasn't going to audition anyways.

That same night I went home and my father said to me, "Son, why don't you try to join a sports team maybe soccer or basketball or if you'd like you should try cross country?" I handed my father the flyer that my drama teacher had given me and said, "This is what I want to audition for." My father looked at me and said, "Yeah that's great but what about a sports team?" I knew I wasn't good at sports since I had a bad experience in my grade nine gym class. I had thought

STRUGGLING TO BE THE VOICE

about branching into something new and this was my chance. On the back of the flyer, it asked to pick an emotion and speak one line. The line was, "You. Uhh. How could you do that to me?" The emotion I picked was sadness because it seemed to resonate with how I was feeling on the inside. I had rehearsed that line in the mirror over and over until I got it perfect down to the last second. On the day of the audition, I walked into the room with my drama teacher and another teacher from the department who had a serious look on her face. "Go," she said, "You have five minutes." I started to fake a cry and said the line "Youuuu. Uhhhhhh. How could you do that to me?" as I pretended to cry. "Again," she said. I did the line once more. "Again," she said. I did the line for the third time. "Stop," she said to me. She didn't believe me for some reason. Was my willing suspension of disbelief not good enough for her? She stood up and looked at me and said, "Say the line with anger." "What?" I said. "Say the line with the emotion anger. You heard me," she said. I started to yell the line, "You! Uhh! How could you do that to me!" She got up from her desk and stood in front of me, "Ahhhhhh!" She screamed at me. "Let everything come to surface," she said. So I did. I channeled a part of me that was angry. I remembered how I had been beaten, how I had been ridiculed. I remembered all the times I had been silenced. "You! Ahhhhh! How could you do that to me!" I said. As the words began to surface and my emotions began to run high, my heart began to beat louder than it had ever before. I knew for the first time I was letting my anger out and it felt rewarding. "Good willing suspension of disbelief," she told me. I knew it was there too because for the first time I was being myself, channeling the emotions within myself that I had suppressed for many years. She taught me that I wasn't feeling sadness at that moment in my life, it was anger. Somehow she knew I was hiding anger in me. Till this day, I don't know how she knew but that audition changed the way I saw myself. It helped me realize that I wasn't sad, I was angry but didn't know how to express my anger in a healthy way.

STRUGGLING TO BE THE VOICE

THE WATER BOY

I called him the water boy because every day he made sure to pack a few extra water bottles for school. He never drank that amount of water in a day. Whether he would pack five or ten water bottles, it didn't matter because he always saved a couple for me. It happened almost every day in grade four when he would wait for me after school. He would wait at the bottom of the hill with his backpack on the ground and the water bottle cap undone. In each hand he held a water bottle. The caps on both water bottles were undone and his backpack filled with more water bottles was for when he was done with the two water bottles in his hand. Almost every day that year, he would dump water on me as I walked home. It didn't matter if I ran home because he always found a way to chase me down. He was much faster than me so every day I knew that he was going to dump water on me. He would turn two water bottles all the way round and dump them on the top of my head. My school books would get wet and my clothes would be drenched in water. I knew that my cries wouldn't matter because no one would be able to see my tears. All they would see is water.

It wasn't until one day when I came home and fell onto the ground with my wet clothes. As I lay in front of my house, I realized how much pain the water boy caused me. My mom came running outside as my eyes started to water. "Mom, tell me it gets better," my voice cracked. She looked at me and said, "Son, I will always walk the journey with you no matter what." In that instant, I knew that she had already known what had happened. She was upset that he had dumped water on me but she was even more confused why God wasn't there when I needed him. I learned that no matter how difficult your journey be, those who love you will always find a way to walk it with you; they will never walk away from you.

REVENGE

It never got any better with the water boy. Each day he would bring more and more water bottles just for me. Meetings with the school principal didn't do anything, it only made him do it more. Then one day I came up with a plan. I figured out a way for the water boy to leave me alone. I decided to ask my mom to pack me a hot lunch that day. I believe it was chicken soup but I can't quite remember. I went to the cabinet and found the biggest thermos I could find. She went into the kitchen and packed my lunch in the thermos that I had specially picked. I made sure to place my lunch in my blue lunch bag that I always held in my hand. That same day the water boy gave me smiles and a few scratches on my wrist with his nails during class. But I knew, after school was when he would have a surprise waiting for him. So that day after school, I made sure to sneak out of the class early and this time I waited for him at the bottom of the hill. I could see him in the distance looking for me but I knew that he was in for a surprise. He got out his two water bottles as usual and proceeded towards the bottom of the hill. What he didn't know was that I was hiding in the nearest bush and was waiting for him to come down the hill. Before he could undo the caps of the two water bottles, I took my blue lunch bag with my heavy metal thermos in it and wacked him on the head. He fell on the ground momentarily as I started to run home.

In my opinion, it was self-defense but I knew I had reached a breaking point and so my way of standing up was revenge. I went home and told everyone what I had just done because I was proud of it. When I told my mother she looked at me and grabbed my hands. "Son," she said, "hands are for loving not for hitting. You taught me that." I knew then that it didn't feel any better on the inside knowing what I had just done. I knew that when I asked my mom if it gets better it would but revenge was not the way. Revenge was not the way to stand up for myself. Anytime you seek revenge on someone who hurts you, remember that you can never know how to be any different if you never choose to approach circumstances differently with others.

ACCEPTANCE

Her name was Candy, she was my best friend at the time. I had known her from my first school because we met in summer school in my grade nine year. She sat beside me in Mrs. Tran's class who would place her school supplies and monies in a toolbox. I never knew she was my friend until she told me how important I was to her. We hadn't known each other that year. We walked the same hallways, we attended different classes. There were many differences between us. Everyone liked her and for some reason no one seemed to like me. Everyone who disliked me, liked her. I guess it was because she was more popular than me that I felt like our two worlds would never meet. But somehow they did. The summer of grade nine was the summer that I prayed to God and asked God to send me someone who could love me. Someone who wouldn't judge me. Someone who could learn to accept me. That same summer, we met in Mrs. Tran's class where she sat to the right of me in the back corner closest to the door. It was convenient because it was easier to talk without the teacher knowing. "Hi" she said on the first day of class. "Hi" I said. Inside I was hesitant because what she didn't know was that after the following month, I would no longer be attending our school. No one had known that I had transferred because it was my secret that would keep me safe, that would give me the start to my next chapter.

As the semester unfolded, we caught ourselves talking all day and it was good because it helped pass time. What turned into all-day conversations in class became late night calls and video chats. I wasn't sure if she knew what the other kids were saying about me, and I was afraid that if she knew she would stop talking to me because many people had done that to me before. Nightly conversations turned into all-nighters on the phone accompanied with a bag of popcorn. I knew that the friendship wouldn't last forever because I was already removed from the school the following year. But somehow it did. The end of summer was fast approaching so I waited for summer school to finish to decide whether to tell my secret or not. That night I ended up calling her. It was past eleven o'clock but I needed to tell her, urgently. We talked for hours that night and then she said something that changed my life forever. She said, "I love you Nick" and I realized that God had answered my prayer. He had sent someone who would accept me, someone who could love me. I lay down in my backyard on the grass and looked up at the stars. I counted as many stars as I could see that night. I was trying to find the star that didn't seem the brightest and found one surrounded by numerous bright stars. I thought about myself being that dull star and how her light could surround me. I knew then that I had to tell her. "I'm moving schools in September," I said. "What?" she replied. What had I done! No one was supposed to know my secret. It slipped out and the words rolled out of my mouth somehow. "Yeah, I'm not coming back next year. It's too complicated to explain". She was silent for a few moments and then she said the words that changed the way I saw other people. "It's okay. I understand. I know what happened to you, but it's okay because it doesn't matter." She didn't judge me even though she had already known what other kids were saying. She didn't care that my Friday nights were spent going to thrift stores or that at times, I was socially awkward. Suddenly, nothing mattered more to her than being my friend. I knew then that somewhere out there, the universe had listened to my cry for a friend. She has been friends with me nine years later, we both have moved to new chapters in our life, however she always knows that I am only a phone call away.

STAND UP

It was grade eleven when I got the call after school as Candy said, "Hey Nick, can I tell you something?" I knew then that whatever she had to tell me was important because she sounded hesitant, almost afraid because she knew the news she was going to tell me would hurt my feelings somehow. She proceeded to tell me that someone in her law class was telling the other kids, "There was someone named Nick D whom we would call by his last name and he would get upset." What that other boy never told the other kids was that it was more than just saying Nick D. It was terms like "faggot, Dickshaw, Gaylord". It was Facebook posts of their crotch and me being tagged in their photo as their crotch. It was the number of times I tried to kill myself and wouldn't eat and then over eat till I would puke.

STRUGGLING TO BE THE VOICE

That was what I felt. That is what I lived with for years. Candy knew how many years I lived with the pain of bullying that led me down a spiral of misery. She knew the hurt I felt because our phone calls became my escape. She reminded me that I was loved.

Till this day, I believe that every time she said "I love you" she meant it. I believe this because that day she told me, she gave me the voice I didn't have. In front of the whole class she said, "How dare you? Your memory must be short-termed for you to forget all the things you did. You don't know him. You know nothing about him and as a matter of fact, I'm still friends with him till this today." The whole class started to cheer for her as her teacher said, "Good job Candy. That was a nice thing you said about your friend". Candy showed me that sometimes we don't have the power to use our voice to stand up, maybe it's because we don't know how to or because we're afraid to, but there will always be someone who will. Someone out there will give you the voice you deserve. This shouldn't mean that you rely on other people to be your voice but it shows that standing up for yourself or others is the greatest power you have against the darkness. It demonstrates that words can cause a chain reaction. Words can give you the power to stand against anyone who tries to take your voice away.

I HAVE TO WRITE MY TEST

It happened in the summer of my grade eleven year. I was walking to school that morning with my headphones plugged in and my iPod in my left pocket. I was wearing socks with slippers because they felt the most comfortable that day. I had left early for school because I needed time to think. As I started to walk, I started to think about where my life would take me after high school and what kind of career I could pursue. No matter what career I saw myself doing, nothing made me happier than being a teacher at the time so I knew that was probably what I wanted to be. I started to walk alongside the main road that connected the end of my street to my high school. My slippers felt sticky on the bottom. I think it's because the day before I had stepped on gum. As I started to walk alongside the main road, I approached a stoplight. The red hand symbol was blinking rapidly as I waited patiently for the stoplight to display the walk symbol. In just a few minutes, the stoplight turned red and the crosswalk symbol appeared. I looked both ways as I proceeded to walk. The last thing I remember was coming close to the other side of the crosswalk and hearing a car race towards my left. As I turned, I saw a gray car and that was the last moment I remembered before I woke up.

About two minutes later, I remember opening my eyes and being underneath the car but not remembering how I got there. "Oh my, thank goodness you're okay. I'm so sorry I hit you. Let me take you to the hospital," she said. "Hospital?" I thought, for what, nothing was wrong with me. I looked at my body and couldn't find any marks or bruises. There wasn't a scratch on me. I turned and looked at her and said, "I feel fine and I have to go write my test." "Let me take you to the hospital please," she replied. "No really I am okay," I said. Both of us couldn't understand how there were no marks or bruises on my physical body due to the impact of the car hitting my body. "You hit the floor and then I heard a thump," she said. I didn't believe her because there wasn't a mark on me. Besides, my mind was set on my test and that to me was more important at the time. I told her to drop me at school as she went to the police station to file a police report. When I was at school the same lady was in the office and had informed the school what had just happened. "What happened?" the principal questioned. "Oh! I got hit by a car but I'm fine. I told her there was no need calling an ambulance because I wasn't hurt," I told him. When the police showed up later, I ended up having to go to the hospital anyways. When the doctor looked at me he said, "Are you sure you went under the car?" "I'm pretty sure," I said. The police officer went to talk to the lady, "Ma'am, did he go under your car?" "Yes I am certain," she said. "Was he wearing a backpack?" the officer asked. "No, he just had his iPod in his pocket and a few pencils in his left hand," she said. I waited for the doctor to finish examining me. "How do you go under a car and not a mark on you?" he said. I looked at him and said, "I'm missing my Math test." He started to laugh. "Ah. Okay. I don't know what to tell you other than to get lots of rest and yeah." He sent me home that same day.

After I left the hospital, I knew that something made sure I didn't die that day. Something out there wanted me alive but I couldn't figure out why. Someone out there cared for me enough to make sure nothing happened to me. Whatever that someone or something was probably knew how much I was worried about writing my Math test. I knew that whatever had just happened was from above because there was God was saying, "Hello. You matter." I knew then that the universe never leaves us alone. You are always being followed. No matter where you turn somehow God is right behind you. How I survived a car coming off the highway and hitting me is still a question I ask myself.

CHANGE ROOM

It was grade seven when I discovered a way to escape recess. I wanted to escape so that the other kids wouldn't have to see me sitting by myself. I didn't want to put my head down with my back placed against the school's cold brick wall. Playing with pebbles on the ground became very redundant over the many years. One day, as I was walking from the boys' change room I came up with a plan that when recess came, I would sneak into the change room so that I wouldn't have to go outside. So I did that and it became a routine for me. Every day I would wait for the lunch bell to ring and would sneak down the stairs along the side of the school and run into the change room quickly in hopes nobody would see me. I did that almost every day that year and it was one of the most liberating years of my life. In the change room, I found peace because there was no noise like how the playground would be. There was nobody trying to pull my pants down unlike how they were on the playground.

There was only me and this red dodgeball I found hidden in the change room. I found it lying under one of the tiles I had popped up in the change room's ceiling. It happened spontaneously, when I was jumping on the bench inside the change room and had accidently hit the tile with my head, there popped out the red dodgeball. I would kick and throw that red dodgeball and it became fun because there was no one to laugh at me. One day, a teacher found me inside the change room when she saw me running outside the room. That teacher told my teacher and my parents and they got a phone call. "He's been hiding in the change room. Another colleague found him in there," my teacher told my parents. My teacher and parents never knew that I stayed in that change room because I was alone. Days spent in the change room were more peaceful than days spent on the playground.

Eventually, I had to start spending recess outdoors but it never got any easier sitting alone against the side of the school's cold brick wall. Even though I was among so many schoolmates, I spent most recesses alone. What this experience taught me was that to be alone isn't having no one around you, it's the feeling that there is no one around you who cares.

THE GIRL ON THE BLEACHERS

This story starts in my grade eleven year with a girl named Sara who always spent lunch sitting outdoor on the bleachers by herself. Sara had long black hair accompanied with a pair of sweats and a hoodie she wore frequently. I met Sara when I had gone outside one day to spend lunch the same way, by myself. As I approached the bleachers, I saw her sitting alone talking on the phone. She became my friend as the year progressed, but most importantly she reminded me of what being alone felt like.

She always spent lunch outside. It didn't matter how cold or how rainy it was because she would still be outside on the bleachers. For some reason she felt safer outdoors than she did inside. I didn't blame her because indoors was where most of the high school melodrama happened. She was more like me then, I thought at the time, both of us were trying to find any escape. Us trying to avoid as many conflicts with other schoolmates. I never knew Sara was being bullied until one day she told me. "These other girls in my gym class make fun of the way I dress." I knew then what I had experienced a few years prior would be valuable advice for her. Without hesitating I said, "Sara, do you feel alone?" She replied, "Yes." Somehow I was being tested by the universe, and the lesson was, 'what did you learn from being bullied?'. I knew that I had to give Sara the advice that I had learned earlier in my own life. So every lunch I would meet with Sara outside on the bleachers and made sure to dress warm so that I wouldn't be cold when we spent lunches outdoors. I started to wear more sweats and hoodies to make Sara feel like her clothes didn't make her feel different. She wasn't the only one who felt different, so was I. As days turned into weeks and eventually into months, Sara found her confidence. She began to make more friends and she eventually started to spend lunch indoors. Cafeterias used to be the worst place for her because that was where the bullies were, but for some reason it never stopped Sara from being happy.

Sara helped me understand that there is a common underlying human experience we all face at some point and that is feeling lonely. Ironically, it is so common to feel this way and so many of us have people around us, yet no one at times. It makes us feel like we don't have any options when we are stuck trying to cope with struggles in our daily life. It never made sense that Sara never feared me, I thought she should have been afraid because most people saw me and thought, loser. For some reason, she never feared me at all. She found ways to make me feel confident about myself and embrace my pain, by turning it into lessons that I applied towards other people's struggles. Sara made me reflect on my experiences of being bullied and say, "Thank you for the lesson". If I never had the experience, I don't think I would have had the wisdom to help Sara find her confidence.

The girl on the bleachers soon became the girl with all the friends, all the confidence and the one who was liked among most of the teachers. I learned from Sara that deep down we are all searching for the same thing. We all want to be accepted. We all, in some way, are looking for a way to fit in because it is much easier to conform than it is not to. Never feel ashamed of looking different or feeling different than those around you because not everyone will understand why you look a certain way or behave in a certain manner. But who knows there might be someone who will guide you through that difficult time as I had guided Sara.

STRUGGLING TO BE THE VOICE
THE BOY THAT CAME TO THE STALL

It was grade six when she beat me with her ruler in one hand and her fingers curled into a fist in the other. Her name was Tracy and she was what I called the change. She wasn't a bad person, only someone who got caught up in other people's drama. Some of the other kids who disliked me put her up to beating me with her ruler. I remember this story fairly well because that day I realized even the bathroom was not a good hiding spot when you have to cry.

One day, Tracy came into the classroom with a vengeance for me. I wasn't sure why but I saw it in her face. My other classmates laughed because they knew what she was about to do to me without me realizing until she smacked me with her ruler. She pulled out her thirty centimeter ruler and smacked me across my face and across my left arm. I tried to find whatever I could on the ground to throw at her but she was much more intimidating than I was. After she was done, my class started to laugh that was when I ran to the bathroom and locked the stall door as I started to cry. I crept in the corner of the stall with my legs in a upward position and placed my head onto my lap as my tears fell into my jeans. Within a few minutes, one of my classmates popped his head over the stall and said, "Hey Nick, come back to class. It's going to be okay. Don't cry." I never forgot what he did for me because he was one of the only people who told me, "it's going to be okay". He helped make elementary school seem easier because he stood up for me quite often. Even though there were many people who found me as an easy target, he wouldn't let them say anything that would hurt my feelings. Throughout the years, we became casual friends and into high school we stayed that way till I transferred schools and we lost touch. I never forgot how the words "it's going to be okay" were all I needed to pick myself back up.

I learned years later that Tracy was not a bad person; she never wanted to hurt me but whatever someone told her drove her to hit me with that ruler. The boy who came to the stall reminded me that situations arise that make us feel vulnerable but it doesn't mean we can't get back up. It is going to be okay. No matter where you are or whatever you are going through, it is going to be okay. This moment will pass and you will move on, and hopefully one day, you will look back and see the growth and remember to thank your experiences for enlightening you in ways that wouldn't have been possible if they had not occurred.

FRIEND OR FOE

He was a friend in my elementary school who slowly became my enemy once he started to realize that other people disliked me. He was always kind to me until one day he and another girl wacked me with a skipping rope they had found on the playground. I never forgave him because he had found a way to smile at everyone but I knew that underneath that smile, there were lies and deception. Everyone seemed to believe that smile on his face because that smile never left. It seemed like he got happiness from inflicting pain on others. Much like the boy who had tried to hurt my sister when I was younger, somehow pain equaled happiness for him. He was what they called your friend or your foe. You never really knew what you were to him because he would make you wait to find out and you knew you were the foe by his behavior towards you, if he would tease you or spread rumors about you. I always tried to avoid him because I was afraid of being on his bad side, even though I already was. Even though he and I never really got along, I will say that years later, I think he found a way to learn from his faults with me.

Years later when in my grade nine gym class, he would watch as the other boys would tease me. One day he waited till everyone was gone to say to me, "Are you okay?" That was the first day I realized that he wanted to change for the better, that he had learned from his experiences. He was just like me, learning lessons in life to become a better person each day. Even if it did take him many years, he eventually understood the lesson. The lesson was that change helps us learn from our faults, faults help us learn from change.

STRUGGLING TO BE THE VOICE
PATHS THAT CROSS

Most of us have at least one teacher who inspired us somehow. Whether it be through class discussions as they sat on the front desk, or after class when you would go for extra help. Somehow they had an influence on you and you are always reminded of how they influenced you. That is the influence they had. The ability to never give up on you, to share with you all the wonderful things you could not see in yourself.

Her name was Dr. Lou. Till this day, she has influenced me to listen to my inner calling and trust it. That has led me to write this book. She always had this laugh that you could hear at the end of the hallway and her desire to teach was admirable. I remember having her for numerous classes because she would always run into the class at just the right time with a cup of Tim Hortons coffee and a red pen behind her right ear. She was the mother I never knew I needed until I moved away from home to pursue my studies and that is why her influence has been impactful. I was being guided on my journey without even realizing that God had already aligned the right people in my path who would influence me in a positive way.

It was towards the end of my final year when I decided that I needed to let her know how much of an impact she had on me. So I decided to let her know because gratitude is one of the greatest gifts you can give to one another. I titled it "The Influence You Have" and it read something like this.

THE INFLUENCE YOU HAVE

There is something so wonderful about you. You find happiness and joy in the smallest things that help you embrace the world around you. For the last few years, I have been away from my family and friends and have taken chances to pursue new aspirations. I did not know I would be at this point in my life. That I would meet people along my path who could bring joy in all that they do. In fact, it was so unclear to me that I would even pursue Math as a major. Yet, I felt mothered by you and you encouraged me to pursue my passion. Your heart has always shown in all that you do. In all that you do, you must be your truest self because the greatest influence you can have on others is living your authentic self. You are the image of an everlasting nurturer overflowing with kindness that you shed on those around you.

My mother once told me that there are no accidents. That the people whom we encounter presently and later in life are people who come into our lives to teach us at least one thing, and even then we can take a greater lesson and purpose from every experience. If there is one thing I have learned from you, it is that kindness and compassion can take you much further in this life. Over these last four years, I have not only become much more knowledgeable but have become insightful on how to live a purposeful life, and have had the joy of being accompanied by you along my journey. You have a way of reminding me that I am enough because I have been told that I do not have the capability. That I cannot be my true self because being me is not enough. Despite this, thank you for taking a chance on me and reminding me that in all that I do, I am enough.

WHISPER FROM ABOVE

There are people in this world who make it their life's work to discourage. Many will define me in ways that will undermine what I can do. But you have been one of the greatest gifts these past four years as you have helped me find purpose. I would like you to know that your assurance and encouragement has kept me hopeful. I hope that there is a time where I can show those around me the same compassion that you showed me. When that day comes, I will always be reminded of the influence you have had on me. I have many years ahead of me and yet I will remember people like you who have given me hope. I will remind myself of my mother's words when she said we can learn at least one thing from every experience, from every encounter. Many years will come from now and my life will take different turns, maybe someday we will meet again or someone will remind me of your kindness and compassion.

CHAPTER NINE

Find Your Voice

TRANSGENDER AND SPIRITUALITY

As the world is progressing into higher states of consciousness, many of us are lost in trying to understand why so many young people are living freely, unapologetically, and authentically. Within this category, we see people who identify as LGBTQ+ or without labels. In these communities, you are likely to find people who identify as transgender. In this we have a lot of people who are confused with their lifestyle because they believe it is based on choice and then there are those who believe it is not choice. From a spiritual perspective, sexuality is not a choice but is more of awareness and understanding. Consider that the world we live in is made up of duality. That there are two sides to everything, so for every up there's a down and for male there's a female, like opposites. Now knowing this is true, what we classify as male or female is solely an energy. For example, if you paint your nails and wear makeup you are considered a hyper version of femininity energy. Vice versa for males as well but our understanding of gender and sexuality is shifting. A female who wears sweat pants and has a deeper voice does not fit the hyper feminist category and that is nature's way of saying we are different for a reason. Now establishing that everyone has male and female energy but at different levels, we are now starting to understand that gender is no longer rigid and sexuality is not a reflection of gender.

Sexuality is the soul's desire to look for new experiences with people who can teach them how to grow their male or female energy. If you believe in reincarnation then you will probably resonate with this theory. Let's say a soul reincarnates in the last ten lives as female, so there becomes a strong identification with the female gender. Now in the next life following these last ten lives, the soul incarnates as a male. Now this person feels an identity loss because they disassociate themselves from their physical body. So their expression might be somewhat hyper feminist such as wearing makeup, heels, and dresses. The expression we see in a transgender identity is the identification and expression of who they truly are. Although they are born male, they might identify as something else and that really is okay because identification with physical form does not mean you have to be male or female. Spiritually, it means that your soul understands it exists beyond the physical form. Whatever your identity is or however you choose to not define yourself is okay. What it demonstrates is that you understand you come from something greater and there is a knowing in you that you exist beyond physical form and so your human experience should not be limited to identity rather your human experience should explore identity.

WOMEN AND SUPPRESSION

We all perform gender because we have been told that we need to fit into society and if we do not fit into society, we are fearful. This fear is because we are afraid that being outside of the norm means that we do not conform to the social constructions of society.

Historically, women have been stereotyped as passive, immersed within themselves. Conversely, male dominance is seen as active, creative, productive, and powerful. Throughout history, these two forces have denied women the right to power within society. This stands to show that women have a hard time reaching power because of these social constructions that mark women as inferior beings.

The repetition throughout history for a woman to be the childbearing and childrearing figure has put limitations on their ability to perform outside of her nature's duty. Thus, women are restricted by repetition to perform as a nurturing figure. The stigma around reproductive labour has existed throughout history as her contribution to society was based on her pregnancy and ability to reproduce. Social stigmas today reflect the historical notion that women are powerless in a male-dominated society. You hear comments like "women belong in the kitchen" or you see rich, powerful men use their privilege and power as a way to keep women silent. The call for women to be more represented in a society and culture that has suppressed them for too long is now. As we move away from historical ways of thinking about women and household duties, in today's culture women hold everyday jobs. Many women have the chance to overcome the stigmas that they have been rooted in for so long. Let us help build a world in which women are represented to the utmost degree. They have lost their voice in a world that gives them none.

SEX VS. GENDER

Similarities between sex and gender are different in their nature because gender is a dominating aspect of life. Conversely, sex is something that is unchanged because it is a part of one's self and individuals have the choice to reject their biological sex through hormone replacement therapy and other means. Gender is changeable because behaviors related to your sex may change due to societal impacts. Gender can be adopted by men and women and characteristics that define gender stereotypes can be interchangeable between the two sexes. Performance of gender is a construction of gender because we are expected to be a certain way. Society expects that the only constructs that exist are male and female. This must exist and if we do not perform gender, then we are not performing gender roles. Everyone performs gender and follows their gender identity because one cannot express who they really are because they are following the universal rules of society; to perform gender.

WOMEN, SEX, AND GENDER

Our biological sex and social influences make us choose particular roles of either male or female because the two sexes are all we identify within society. Individuals who do not accept their roles become excluded from society because they do not perform as male or female. To silence women, we have constructed gender in a way that makes them seem inferior to males. Everyday culture undermines the social and cultural values of womanhood and sex. For example, language is rooted in a masculinist way of thought. Words like "mankind" in relation to all people. This suggests that women are inferior beings in comparison to a world that is dominated by "man".

HETROSEXUAL NORMS

In today's culture, there is a misconception that non-heterosexual relationships must reflect the dominate and submissive standards. The dominate in relation to the male and the submissive in relation to the female companion. Homosexuals and other relations are thought to follow the same mentality. Everyday culture easily assumes that if two males are together, one must be submissive and the other dominant. This mentality reflects the heteronormative way of thinking that there must be a power structure in the relation in which one plays the role of inferior. This is problematic because as long as society still has this perception of power in relationships, equality between the two sexes will be much harder to reach. Once we break down the power structure mentality in relationships, we can start to move closer towards equality and represent women fairly and accurately in society.

POWER STRUCTURES

Power structures teach us that in order to reach universal love we need to break down old ways of thinking. By deprogramming ourselves of a power structure mentality, we can begin to see women not as inferior but as equal. Spiritually, we are learning that these power structures are an egoistic way of feeling superior. These structures only exist to blind us from the truth. The truth being that there is nothing a man can do that a woman can't. We told ourselves that women aren't as strong as men or smart because that is what we have learned over generations of suppression.

We must look at what has happened historically and realize that suppression has never worked. Suppression of blacks or African Americans led to more pain, more internal hurt. Suppression of women and objectification of women are not a path that will help us reach equality. Historically, women were considered men's property. Now culture is changing and women have moved away from being labeled as property, and instead are owning properties of their own.

STRUGGLING TO BE THE VOICE
POVERTY: A CONTINUOUS CYCLE

Poverty is people living in poor conditions due to the lack of access to those resources within society and not being able to obtain those resources. The Karl Marx theory says that there are two main classes within society - the bourgeoise and the proletariat. The bourgeoise is the capitalist class and the proletariat is the working class who have a much lower income. He says that in society, you have different working classes where some benefit financially more than others. The working class put in their physical labor while the capitalists, also known as owners, make profit from the working class. Poverty is caused from the discrepancies between the two classes within society and the rich benefiting from the labor of the working class. Poverty still exists today because it is hard to have this American Dream when you do not have the fundamentals of education, a job, housing, etc. In the modern era, we have resources to help people move out of poverty into the working community but unfortunately poverty still exists.

If we consider poverty on a macro level versus micro level, we can consider all possible effecting and contributing factors leading to the cycle of poverty. The cycle of poverty exists due to families, individuals, poor and sick who have become either relatively poor or absolutely poor leading to their children in poverty, and their children's children in poverty. This creates a cycle of poverty. The massive gap between the rich and poor in Marxian's theory shows how the wage gap has led to cycles of poverty that has continued to exist over the years.

Issues such as gender inequality or sexual orientation have become more aware in society. People are beginning to understand that there are individuals who are lesbian, gay, transsexual, etc. If we create more awareness about poverty then individuals would not be afraid to talk or express the subject matter.

Someone who works twenty hours can be paid less than someone who works eight. Now this could be due to the fact that the under privileged in society are forced to do low income jobs. To ensure this does not happen, we should create an equilibrium to reduce the wage gap that exists. By doing this, we can reduce the negative factors that poverty leads to.

INDIGENOUS COMMUNITIES

In today's economy, we draw towards a Western way of life. Thus, losing the value of culture from our ancestors because we have become infatuated and familiarized to a Western way of life. However, Western culture suppresses the values of indigenous customs and traditions by a rapid economy that continues to immerse into a Western way of life.

Customs such as oral tradition have been a custom to indigenous people as a way to document their history. Laws were not documented on paper put rather in song or ritual. However, Westernizers who colonized North America did not consider oral tradition, a suitable form of evidence. This is evident because documented and written evidence is considered more legitimate in Western culture.

Conversely, if culture is forced, you do not have the ability to choose. The behavioral expression of indigenous culture was suppressed; as a tool to assimilate them into Western culture. The cultural identity of the indigenous community is a reflection of what they truly identify themselves as. Having to suppress indigenous culture and assimilate into a Western way of life is a misrepresentation of cultural identity. Cultural identity stands as a loss for indigenous people who are living in an environment where Western culture is a dominant way of life; causing them to condition to a Westernized standard of life.

ASSIMILATION

Assimilation is the idea of integrating yourself into a particular culture or society. An example of this is coming from a foreign country into Canada and taking on customs, clothes, and food of that culture or society. Someone who is assimilated within an environment has become adapted to their environment.

Assimilation in North America is subtle and it is challenging for Westernizers in becoming accustomed to immigrants in Canada. Canada has been an admirable example of why cultural identity is crucial at this point in time. Having a gender-balanced cabinet with members of various cultures is an accurate representation of what Canada looks like. We often say that North America is the boy or girl next door and it is. The boy next door has dark skin and the girl next door is mixed with many ethnicities but is Canadian. That is what Canada looks like; people from all over the world who come to one nation and stand as one nation before God.

As people from all over the world migrate to Canada, we see many cultural and religious clothing, jewelry, and other expressions of cultural identity that may be not identifiable with some Westernizers. For example, some Muslim women wear the hijab and members of the Sikh community may wear a metal bracelet both as a symbol of cultural and/or religious identification. When we are not familiarized with the culture or identity of certain communities, we must understand that it is much harder for these communities to exist amongst so many of us that are heavily influenced by Western values. A Western way of life is an entirely new way of life for most immigrants and with this awareness of cultural identity brings understanding and hopefully acceptance of everyone. We have to find awareness in our lives and seek ways of being aware. Awareness is the first step towards change, people have the will to change once they realize there is a problem.

The spiritual lesson in assimilation is acceptance. Just like how we discussed acceptance of all skin colors. As part of Canada's history, indigenous communities were forced to assimilate. We cannot disregard history nor can we live through it but we can live by it as an example to become better with one another. God loves all things and cultural identity is one of his many creations that strives to connect people. Cultural identity brings awareness because we are learning to see that underneath culture and religious identity is humanity.

It teaches us to break down the barriers that separate us from one another. It shows us that culture is just an expression of love through family, food, belief, and inspiration. We are all searching for a way to feel more connected to one another, and cultural identity bridges that connection to one other.

PRIDE AND SPIRITUALITY

It was my second year of university and I was going to attend my first Pride. I never really knew anything about the LGBTQ+ community but I was willing to learn. It started with a friend of mine who had come out earlier that year and invited me to attend Pride with them. Pride exceeded my expectations and members of the LGBTQ+ community have a way of making you feel at home. The community doesn't care who you are or what color your skin is, or how masculine or feminine you are because they understand that our differences only divide us if we allow them to separate us. That is what the fight for Pride is, under all the colors of the rainbow they are saying we are here and we exist. I never understood that until I made a friend at Pride that year who taught me we are more alike than different. I never really knew much about the

LGBTQ+ community growing up in a Catholic school and then years later, going to a school where there weren't a lot of people who identified themselves as LGBTQ+. My knowledge was very limited but it didn't stop me from learning. "Happy Pride" people said to me as they walked by. So I started to say the same thing. "Happy Pride," I started to say to everyone who I had met. Even if there were people just passing by me briefly, I was saying "Happy Pride" to everyone. I'm pretty sure my friend got a little annoyed of me but I was excited.

Then something happened that evening that changed the way I saw other people. It was at one of the outdoor concerts when I said "Happy Pride" and someone who identified himself as a male named Jacob turned around wearing a crop top and shorts. I immediately put my arms around him and said "thank you". He hugged me back but didn't really know why I said thank you. For me, the "thank you" was because he showed me that he wasn't different he was told he was different by a society based on constructions and labels. I immediately thought about that girl in my grade seven class who told me I was different because of the food I ate and so I believed her. Jacob wasn't different, he was just like you or me but had to wake up each day trying to be himself in a world where being different is still a challenge against the masses.

Members attending Pride were finding their voices by saying things like "We're here and we're queer". That was their way of saying "see us, hear us because we are not going anywhere". For the first time, I saw people who didn't want to conform, who weren't willing to step outside being anything but themselves to be accepted. They were showing people that they too are no different from other communities. If they are labeled as different, it was only because people told them they were. That day I learned more about inclusion, authenticity and pride to be who you are regardless of what the status quo tells you to be. Pride taught me that we are more the same than we are unalike. Underneath the clothes and the physical aspects of each other, we are all trying to find our voice in the world. Pride was not about being separate from one another but it was about coming together as one community, LGBTQ+ or not. God makes no mistakes and there is no restriction of how to be happy. So we create restrictions in our lives which stop us from living the life that we were meant to live. God wants everyone to be happy. Even if people do not agree with the way you choose to live your life, don't deny yourself of being yourself and be proud of who you are because love has no limits. If there were any limits, it is because others placed them on us or we placed them on ourselves.

PUPPET MASTERY

It was grade twelve when I had learned about puppets in my drama class. We were learning about how puppets are always controlled by a puppet master. You move your hand gestures or speak and the puppet copies you; the only thing is that no one can see you controlling the puppet, behind the curtain. This made me think how similar it is to the way we see the world today. How many of us are puppets being controlled by puppet masters without realizing that we are? There is an underlying conformity that we don't even realize. For example, the clothes that you are limited to by a certain style or a certain design, alongside this the advertisements for these clothes are continuously being shown to you. It's much easier to buy a pair of clothes than it is to make your own, so most of us conform. The clothes you wear influence how other people see you or the job that you have reflects how high or low your income level is. As puppets, we don't realize that there are people who operate behind the curtain, who influence the way we see each other. When we fight with each other, what we don't often realize is that behind the curtain there is a puppet master that has a heavy influence on the way we see ourselves.

The way we interact with one another is how we acquire new knowledge. This has been done throughout history and is present in today's society. When you become accustomed to your environment, you start to act or behave like your environment. Somehow the environment you are in influences the way you see yourself and the way you perform in society. Who would you be if there was no puppet master behind the curtain? Even the words that you speak at times might be common phrases like "treat others the way you want to be treated" and you learn that because you are taught so by your teachers and peers. Let's say for example, you like to be smacked. Does that make it okay for you to smack other people because that is the way you like to be treated? We don't really question phrases like this because we assume that the context is a positive one. But underlying these common phrases could be the result of a puppet master. Some of us will utilize this phrase as a way to be better with one another and others might take this quote as a way to be obscured without realizing it.

SOCIAL MEDIA

Social Media allows for us to connect to each other anywhere in the world. The advantage of social media is that it allows for people to follow their friends and family through experiences that are documented on their Social Media pages. The connection between people on social media is limited to a screen and a keyboard. In such a busy economy, the amount of time we spend interacting with people beyond the screen is decreasing, leaving us more disconnected from each other now than we ever have been before. There is a misunderstanding that through social media, if you send a message or create a post, everyone can see it and stay connected with you. However despite this, information can be skewed because of biases and misunderstandings of the content you post. Someone might openly disagree and they may post about their opinion of your post. The main problem is the tone in which we write our words. If you make a post and use all capitals, some people might assume that you were upset or angry about the subject manner of your post. If you make a post and skip a few words, the context of what you wanted to say is not what you meant to convey. Words matter and they influence people. When our words are distorted, social media no longer remains a place of freedom of speech but instead freedom of hate. Let us try to improve the way we interact with each other beyond the screen so that we can have the right discernment of each other.

CHPATER TEN

Be the Voice

PURPOSE

When I was in my last year of school, I no longer wanted to study Math because I had a heightened interest in subjects like religion and philosophy. Looking back at the signs, it was clear that I needed to get out of academia and pursue the next chapter of my life, but I didn't listen to my inner voice. It wasn't until the day of my graduation when I realized what I had thought as my purpose in life, wasn't I thought a career in Math would be what I was called to do but it turned out to be a lie I told myself. I didn't know until I walked across the stage, the day of my graduation and felt incomplete. The moment my degree landed into my hand I knew that this was not where I was meant to be in my life.

BE THE VOICE

What was strange about my graduation was that from my first year, all I had dreamed about was walking across the stage and seeing my mother's face in the crowd. I wanted to make her proud. I wanted her to feel like her sacrifices in life meant something. From my first year till my last year of University, I would lie on my bed replaying trailers of people walking across the stage receiving their degrees. I had wanted to seize that moment ever since but when I had that moment, it didn't feel like I had envisioned it. As I was on the stage and the parents were in the audience, I heard my mother's voice, "You are my sweetheart." That was my nickname she called me. All I wanted to say back was, "Thank you for believing in me, mom. All those years in the basement, all the struggles, all the late nights spent because no matter how many people doubted me, you didn't." My degree did not validate who I was going to be in the world, instead it gave me the tools that I needed to use in the world. Our eyes teach us to see, our spirit teaches us to sense. Our hands teach us to touch, our spirit teaches us to feel. Our legs teach us to walk, our spirit teaches us to trust. I now understand that there is a purpose to every problem and a plan to every solution.

DEAR CANDY

Throughout the years, Candy became my hope for the chance of having a true friend. I never felt judged because she was open to understanding me when others weren't. When I talked about her, I wanted to smile because she was one of the first persons who helped me understand what happiness felt like. As the years went by, our late night phone calls turned into all-day coffee runs. Our conversations throughout high school and university turned into talks about spirituality. She always asked, "What is this crazy thing, called life"? But I never really had an answer because I too was stuck trying to work on myself. I was struggling to find myself through the weight of the world. Seeking answers to spirituality would only bring more questions than it would answer. Till this day, she and I both agree that somehow the universe brought the two of us together. That somehow in Ms. Tran's class, we both found ourselves that year. It's a strange thing when even one person in your life can change your life forever. Someone who you may have been friends with, who would have had such a profound impact on your personal growth. I never thought that I would ever be able to pick myself up but she always found a way to remind me that I could. She always reassured me that she would always love and support me no matter where I was in the world, no matter how different our lives might be. As years went by, we created memories with just the two of us. Like our treasure box we had made to late night campfires when she would roast raw bananas and apples.

Somehow whatever was out there in the universe knew that we needed each other. It understood that as much as I needed her to help me heal, she needed me to give her the right words when life left her feeling broken. Our friendship is unlike anything I had ever known because it ranged from going downtown Toronto to making friends with strangers anywhere we went. Candy reminded me that there is a lot more light in the world than there is darkness. That even though so many of us feel disconnected from one another, there is someone out there who will inspire you to live the life you deserve. Someone who will remind you how we all play a role in this human experience, how we all are connected. Candy was the reason I no longer believed in accidents because years later I feel much more alive, free and authentic then I did nine years ago.

THANK YOU MOM

Words cannot describe how much I love you. You always taught me to fight for what I wanted and to never give up. Till this day, I still do. Though every day I face the struggle of insecurity. You taught me to see the light that I could not see alone. You taught me to love myself so that others could learn to love me too. Thank you for being my inspiration and the reason I wake up with a smile each and every day. Thank you for showing me that life can be so wonderful with the people we love and the memories we create. I have never stopped loving you Mom, because love is precious especially when it comes from you. You never stopped loving me and caring for me. Thank you for being part of the process of making me who I am today. Never give up Mom because struggle only makes us stronger. I love you Mom.

INSPIRATION

A lot of people lose their passion and feel out of touch because they forget what inspired them in the first place. A lot of people need to hold onto faith and remember how they got to where they are now.

All I wanted was for someone to understand me, to love me. Everywhere I turned, I felt misunderstood and judged and because of this it made me isolate myself from the world. I just wished that there would be a day where someone would notice me. Where someone would hear my screams. For someone to sense my struggles. What I didn't expect in my life was to be happy because I never thought I was deserving of being happy. I felt that way because too many times I had been hurt. So I became so used to being hurt and manipulated. It made me be known as the naive person;

someone who is weak. I could never find the words to stand up for myself when I was being bullied. I could never find the strength to love myself and defend me.

As long as I started to love me, people started to see that I was authentic and genuine. I guess I never thought I deserved happiness because of the environment I grew up in. Every day was hard for me. People kept calling me names. So I tried to fit in, but no matter how hard I tried, it never worked for me because I somehow found a way to be different. I would hang around with girls because that is where I felt safe. That is where I felt non-judged and the most loved. Love all parts of you because you are created in the image of God. We are here to be a demonstration of love to one another. Walk through life knowing that you are always cared for. When you feel alone, know that you were created and your existence was never an accident.

You were created in the image of God because He believed that you mattered. God created all things but he created you as one of those things and that has never been a mistake. So whether you are a person of color or you identify as LGBTQ+ or you don't identify as anything that is no accident. You are beginning to understand that love sees no color or has no gender because love is love. It is infinite and it speaks to the heart. That is the true essence of who we are. That is the image of God. That is the person who you should wake up in the morning with because you walk that journey with you each and every day.

Too many times, we lose our way in life because of the social conditioning that teaches us what to think. In sight of this, we lose ourselves trying to conform, trying to be someone we are not. So we lose the essence of our true spiritual being that we truly are, a walking example of love. That is who Jesus was and who Gandhi was and the Buddha because God saw no race or religion; he sent them all here to demonstrate to humanity how kindness can trigger compassion. Because of this, it led millions till this day to stand in the light of God.

We are all trying to discover ourselves through our experiences. We are on a path of self-discovery and spirituality. Even if you don't realize it whether you are religious or not. Whether you classify yourself as atheist or as someone who doesn't believe in coincidences. There is a purpose to every experience and a chance to extend your consciousness through every lesson. So what do you do when you are going through something that makes you feel stuck? You try to decipher what the lesson is and learn the lesson to move forward. Everyday keep learning, keep living. You are here because you matter. Science will say you exist because you are made up of matter but God says you exist because you matter.

Within every experience is a spiritual lesson, a lesson that allows for spiritual growth. Just how you train your physical body, you are being trained and molded by experiences for your spiritual self. It is no accident that you are constantly changing. Who would you be if the world never labeled you as a name or classified you as a gender? What is really out there beyond the clouds that place which we don't really think about? If the world never taught you who you were, you would exist beyond any label, beyond any definition of you because you are spirit. You are here because you play a role in the spiritual growth of the planet. If you could be anyone, be yourself because the labels that exist are not really you; they are just what you have been taught to believe about yourself. So connect to the heart space of yourself. Trust that compass that guides you and listen to intuition and instinct because it comes from a place greater than we both know. In life, there are more unknowns than there are answers. That is why life itself is a mystery because there is no guideline of how to live it, to experience it. All you can do is live a life that you feel is fulfilling in whichever way that may be.

A life filled with lessons is a life full of wisdom, and with wisdom you have the knowledge to learn from your mistakes. Knowledge that you would have never known had you not had that experience. That is why when you ask someone if they regret having an experience, most people usually say the experience made them a better person. The experience did not change them, it only enlightened them to make better choices and to teach those around them. That is why we don't regret most of our experiences but when we do it is usually because the lesson from that experience was not learned. In this case, we do not grow spiritually and we do not understand the purpose behind the lesson.

WHY DON'T YOU LOVE ME?

So I don't really know how to tell you this because a lot has happened this past year and we both have been through a lot. I really do try to make things better. I try to hold you to show you that I care. I try to smile and laugh so that you can embrace happiness with me. I try to get along so that we both can grow old together and look back at something so silly. It hurts me every day knowing that someone who played such a big role in my life is no longer there. You don't know how much I looked up to you growing up. You had the love you needed, friends, good grades, confidence and happiness. Much of what I wished I had. No matter how many times people tried to bring me down, you were one of the only people who stood up for me.

Some nights I cried myself to sleep because I didn't know who to turn to or where to go. When you feel like you can't turn to family, friends, or people outside, where do you go? As I get older I learn so much more about myself. I learn that I am amazing and I won't let anyone hurt me again. It's hard for you to understand how much underlying pain I have. I just want you to understand that you are not the only one who has faced struggle. Believe me it gets better. I want to have you in my life so that I would know that no one could hurt me again. I want to feel loved by you even till this day.

PRAYER

When faith is tested, we cannot prevail if we do not learn from the lessons the universe is trying to teach us. Having the courage to do what we aspire to and possessing the faith to carry out one's beliefs is all you need to live a life full of happiness and blessings. Sometimes when we fall, it takes us a moment to acknowledge that God has somehow carried us so that we will always be carried no matter what circumstance life presents us with. Every time I feel alone, I always feel liberated knowing that God looks after me. Even though life may be unfair and uncontrollable, I know that from bottom of my heart faith is all one needs, to have the belief that anything is possible. I am so sorry that in times of selfishness and personal pleasure I turned away from the greatest gift of my life.

I am sorry for the times of my own selfishness I neglected you even though you never chose not to neglect me. I want you to understand that I wanted to fit into a world where people are consumed with egoistic gains of money and power. Lord, help me to understand my intention in all of my momentary actions. Help me to pursue my passion and your will for me. I promise you that I will carry out your destined plan for me if you allow me to. I promise that I will help and nurture and love others as you have loved me.

Lord, I allow you to use me as the intention to fulfill your great plan. If you allow me to do this, I will be forever happy. I am sorry for not realizing how much you love me even though you remind me every day.

BE THE VOICE

SPIRITUAL AWAKENING

Those of you who have had a spiritual awakening probably have a better understanding of who you are. You wake up to the truth of why you are here and how everyone and everything is connected. Spiritual awakening brings awareness of who you are and what purpose you serve in the world. For many of us, online videos, forums, and books can help us understand what a spiritual awakening is. It is not commonly talked about in everyday life, however more and more people are starting to wake up to the truth of their existence. They are starting to understand that we all play a role in the collective consciousness of the universe. Everyone who experiences a spiritual awakening experiences it differently, but once you have the experience you start to realize the significant role your ego plays in disconnecting yourself from the energy source of God. If you have had an awakening or are going through one, know that there are more people who have come into the world to help bring their light to guide you. We cannot let the ego win. Bring as much light into the world. You are here because you matter.

STRUGGLING TO BE THE VOICE

Those of you who have not had a spiritual awakening, remember that God is from within. Look from within yourself to find the answers you seek. Utilize prayer, walk in nature, visualize yourself connected to the earth and connect yourself to the spiritual energy that is all around us.

THE GIFT OF LIFE

When life offers gifts, God offers an even greater gift. Throughout my life, friends, family, and people who I have known have come and gone, making me feel frustrated, angry, and hurt in myself and others. I was taught to respect others to be respected and to love others to receive love. Yet my whole life I have done that. Doing what I was told to do rather than what I wanted to do. I tried my best to fit in, to feel as though I could be a part of something that mattered more. Being a part of something greater than yourself makes you feel special. At the same time, no matter how special you feel I was always so special. The people around me were the ones who enforced that love and respect upon me. Then you realize that it takes a stronger person to stand alone, to hold their head up high because they are enough. It takes a stronger person to smile with confidence. No matter who tells you that you are never enough, know that you are. When people walk out of your life in search of their own lives, do not shed any tears or belittle yourself. God made you as his gift and there are greater gifts in which you are destined to discover.

ALL THINGS CONNECTED

It was a sunny summer day when I and Candy decided to walk through the forest. We found this trail that led us to this oak tree that had somehow tipped over and now leaned above the lake. Its roots were still connected to the ground and it still had life, it just had fallen over the lake. It was the most beautiful thing I had ever seen, like something you would see in a movie. The sun was about to go down as we climbed onto the tree and sat on it leaning above the lake as we dipped our toes in the water. When I looked down, in a moment there was a swarm of fish that was swimming around us in the water. They looked like they were excited to see us. They weren't afraid of us at all for some reason. I turned and looked at Candy and said, "Don't you ever wonder why God created all things like trees, fish, us?" She looked at me and said, "No because I just go with the flow." "No, seriously think about it. What is giving this tree life or the animal's consciousness? How are we all connected?" "All things are connected," she said. I looked at the fish below my feet and realized that they were near me because they had some sort of consciousness. I looked at the tree and realized that the leaves were still green and stared at the sun and how it was about to set. "All things connected," I thought. Somehow I felt she was right, what if all things were connected but we told ourselves that we were more superior to one another or that humans are more superior to animals and so on. That wouldn't make animal cruelty okay.

What if we fooled ourselves to believe that we were separate from one another but the reality is that we are one of the same. We all come from the same place, the same place that connects us to the sun and the trees and the fish and each other. Somehow there is a reason your heart beats and mine beats too. We might not ever be able to figure out how connected we really are, but I know that you have life and the trees and the animal's live means that somehow you know you are more connected to the world than we think. Our connection to one another goes beyond language and how we interact with one another. It stems from our spirituality that is shown in our creative process through dance, music, and prayer. It connects us to one another more than we think because these processes allow us to bring out creativity that comes spontaneously. The universe is more than just scientific; it is also creative. The way the stars are aligned and the way time is synchronized, is both a creative and mathematical process.

Fibonacci numbers are a great example of this; they are a series of numbers that follow a sequence such as 2, 4, 6, 8; where every digit is two more than the previous one. The Fibonacci sequence is a series that consists of the numbers 0, 1, 1, 2, 3, 5… Where each digit is a sum of the previous two digits. For example, the number three comes from the sum of one and two, the two digits preceding three. What makes the Fibonacci numbers interesting is that every number in the sequence is in some way connected to nature. For example, we may see three petals on a flower or leaves arranged in a form of threes. The Fibonacci sequence is both logical and creative in the way we see nature, we see the creative aspects but the way we understand nature is the logical aspect. The Fibonacci numbers demonstrate that the universe is both logic and creativity, more specific scientific and spiritual; when both are used intertwined with one another, the results are beautiful.

FLOWERS THAT BLOSSOM

As I sum up the contents on this book, it is important to remember that mistakes are trying, failing and reflecting on those mistakes again. Know that what may seem like a mistake is only the universe's way of leading us to wherever we are meant to be. Somehow we are brought together by God to experience life in both creative and logical ways. You and I both are a part of the universe's design. My journey from elementary school till now has taught me that life might seem like a roller coaster but there really are wonders and mysteries in life if we are open to learning about them. Question yourself each day as to why you are here because you too deserve answers. We might not ever get closer to the truth but it helps us understand that we are not as different as we think we are.

As I look back on my experiences, I understand that the life I was living is not the life I wanted but it was the life that I needed to experience to give me the wisdom, open wounds, failures, and hurt that were essential to my growth. Just like how a flower blossoms, I could have never blossomed without having been nurtured and watered by those around me.

FINDING YOUR VOICE

Everyone's story deserves to be shared. It is the truth of who you are and that deserves to be told. Your story is how many times you laughed, how many times you cried. It is a crazy diary or journal of yourself that is filled with dreams and desires.

As I sit here and try to understand all that has happened throughout my life, I know now that every chapter in my story played a part in the evolution of my spiritual growth. What started as a cry for help translated years later as an adult who has learned many lessons and taken many detours in life. If you too are struggling to find your voice remember that finding your voice takes time, it takes patience.

Sometimes not knowing what we should do next in our lives gives us a chance to explore ideas that we may be uncertain about. Uncertainty is beneficial because it allows us to explore the things that we have been curious about and it puts us in a position where we have to act in the present moment and make the best decision for ourselves to move forward.

BE THE VOICE. TAKE ONE STEP FURTHER

Remember the following lessons; firstly, your tears never fall because God is there to lift them up.

Secondly, we never really lose someone because they still exist in the hearts of those who remember them. Thirdly, your life can be a beautiful life if you don't fight the lessons life is trying to teach you. Fourthly, life teaches us forgiveness by wounds that never heal until we do. Fifth, life is internal because it is how we live from within ourselves that determines how we perceive life externally. Sixth, speak from your soul so that your words can speak to the heart. Seventh, anyone who has ever lost themselves understands themselves more than those who haven't. Eighth, uncertainty allows us to explore our curiosity. Ninth, there is a purpose to every problem and a plan to every solution. Lastly, no two stories are the same and that is why every story matters. Thank you for letting me be heard and hopefully, this will inspire you to find your voice in a world where it may seem like you have none. Be the voice and take one step further.

References

Antony, Wayne. *Power and Resistance: Critical Thinking about Canadian Social Issues, Sixth Edition.* Fernwood Publishing Co., Ltd., 2017.

New American Standard Bible: Containing the Old and New Testaments. T. Nelson, 1990.

Tolle, Eckhart. *A New Earth: Awakening to Your Life's Purpose.* Penguin Books, 2016.

Made in the USA
Lexington, KY
29 May 2019